Fashioned by God is full of fashion tips and spiritual inspiration that will help you develop a beautiful, rewarding relationship with Jesus.

— Angie and John Thurman, senior leaders, Premier Designs

Being in the world while not of it is a challenge for today's Christian woman. In *Fashioned by God*, author Kathryn Graves helps us not only learn more about wardrobe, accessories, and making the most of what we have, but she also helps us better understand and appreciate our beauty through the eyes of God, who loves what he sees.

—Anita Agers-Brooks, author of *Exceedingly: Spiritual Strategies for Living on Purpose, with Purpose, and for an Abundant Purpose* and *Getting Through What You Can't Get Over*; speaker; common trauma expert; certified personality trainer; business-and-life coach

As a fashion consultant, pastor's wife, and Bible study teacher, author Kathryn Graves understands the multifaceted needs of women. In this devotional book, Kathryn addresses women's fashion concerns and encourages her readers to consider their emotional and spiritual needs.

—Karen Jordan, speaker and author of *Words That Change Everything*

You will love *Fashioned by God*. Drawing on her years of experience in the fashion industry, Kathryn Graves shares organizational ideas, eye-opening fashion tips, and spiritual applications to help us clear the junk from our hearts so we can become the beautiful women God has designed us to be.

—Michelle Cox, author of the When God Calls the Heart series; WhenGodCallstheHeart.com

Fashioned by God will challenge you, make you laugh, encourage your heart, and leave you and your closet more stylish than ever! Kathryn Graves is an incredible woman who shares her heartfelt advice in this one-of-a-kind book. I will definitely be sharing it with friends.

—Rosalinda Rivera, international speaker,
author of *Dare to Begin Again*

Kathryn has taken her years of expertise in the fashion industry and created this simple-to-implement style guide that works for every woman. She has also discovered an incredible secret: the condition of our closets often reflects the struggles within our hearts. With a personable and practical style, Kathryn helps us organize, clean out, and bring beauty to both areas of our lives, resulting in the ability to step out of our closets and into life with confidence and joy. If you have to wake up in the morning and get dressed, then this book is for you.

—Erica Wiggenhorn, Bible teacher, author of
An Unexplainable Life and *The Unexplainable Church*

What a joy to read *Fashioned by God*! Kathryn has a way of being transparent and entertaining at the same time. She has a passion for women and inspires her readers to understand that their beauty comes from the only true source within. This is a must read!

—Greta Bost, Premier Designs, Chic 139

Fashioned by God is a great devotional with good fashion advice and spiritual insights. I will recommend this devotional to all women—young and old alike.

—Doris Kelsey, wife of former Kansas State Senator Dick Kelsey

Fashioned by God is a staple for every woman's bookshelf. Kathryn is open and honest about her feelings and guides us to the lessons she has learned through years of study. The scriptural truth that's woven throughout this uplifting book gives it a foundation and timelessness that will speak for years to come. This is definitely a book that I'll purchase to share with others.

—Edie Melson, director of the Blue Ridge Mountains Christian Writers Conference, social media director at *Southern Writers Magazine*, author of *Soul Care When You're Weary, Maiden of Iron, Alone, While My Child is Away, While My Soldier Serves,* and *Connections: Social Media and Blogging Techniques for Writers*

This devotional is delightful, life-changing, and full of practical wisdom. I found not only spiritual strength but also a way to organize my out-of-control closet. Kathryn Graves has done a masterful job of applying spiritual principles to wardrobe issues. This book is not merely about fashion; it challenges women to live with grace and the unchanging characteristics of God. Is there anything more timeless than that?

—Carol McLeod, Just Joy Ministries, author of *Rooms of a Woman's Heart, Defiant Joy, No More Ordinary, Refined, Pass the Joy,* and *Guide Your Mind, Guard Your Heart, Grace Your Tongue*

Once in a while, we all need a style makeover. It's hard to be objective when you are the only visitor to your closet. Reading *Fashioned by God* is like having a personal wardrobe consultant for thirty days. Kathryn is an experienced voice to help clear the clutter and make your wardrobe work for you. She also encourages you to tend the most essential closet you have—your heart. With gentle persuasion, she invites you to look beyond what you wear to fashioning your heart through an intimate relationship with God. This book makes an excellent devotional gift for women of all ages, and will remain on my bookshelf because it is a book that will never go out of style!

—Cynthia Cavanaugh, speaker, life coach,
author of *Anchored: Leading through the Storms* and
Live Bold: A Devotional Journal to Strengthen Your Soul

I love Kathryn's simple approach to our feminine heart through fashion. So often our confidence can be made or broken by our appearance. Kathryn addresses this in a practical manner and takes us beyond the surface to the deepest longing in our heart—the desire for our Creator. She has effectively aligned the practical with the spiritual in a way that will ultimately simplify your wardrobe and life. You will love her thirty-day journey through your closet and into your heart!

—Pauline Meier, executive director, Premier Designs

Fashioned by God

By Kathryn Graves

A 30-DAY DEVOTIONAL

BroadStreet
PUBLISHING

BroadStreet Publishing® Group, LLC
Savage, Minnesota, USA
BroadStreetPublishing.com

Fashioned by God: A 30-Day Devotional

Unless indicated otherwise, all Scripture quotations are taken from the New King James Version. Copyright © 1982 by Thomas Nelson, Inc. Used by permission. All rights reserved. Scripture quotations marked MSG are from THE MESSAGE. Copyright © by Eugene H. Peterson 1993, 1994, 1995, 1996, 2000, 2001, 2002. Used by permission of NavPress Publishing Group. Scripture quotations marked NASB are taken from the New American Standard Bible, © Copyright 1960, 1962, 1963, 1968, 1971, 1972, 1973, 1975, 1977 by The Lockman Foundation. Used by permission.

Stock or custom editions of BroadStreet Publishing titles may be purchased in bulk for educational, business, ministry, fundraising, or sales promotional use. For information, please email info@broadstreetpublishing.com.

Literary representation: Keely Boeving with WordServe Literary
Cover design by Chris Garborg at garborgdesign.com
Typesetting by Kjell Garborg at garborgdesign.com

Printed in China
19 20 21 22 23 5 4 3 2 1

Contents

Foreword

by Shari Braendel

It thrills me to see Kathryn Graves' *Fashioned by God* on the market to encourage Christian women in their outer appearance. I'm especially excited to see Kathryn take on closet organization and how, at the same time, she relates it to the heart and having a spiritual makeover.

I became an image consultant in the 1990s when the trend of making an impact with the right clothes to advance careers was new on the scene. Enter "finding your right colors" through color analysis from *Color Me Beautiful*. Along with image consulting on the rise, the career gained wide acceptance and received major news coverage.

After being trained as a professional color consultant by CMB, my career as an image consultant took off. I was living in Miami, Florida, and began working with female attorneys planning their wardrobes to help them move up in the ranks at their firms. I wrote dress codes for the banking industry and assisted female professionals, along with male clients, to have smart wardrobes.

I became a Christian in my late twenties, and, though successful in my career, God began rearranging my thinking as it pertained to my chosen profession. Though I had a degree in fashion merchandising and was thoroughly enjoying working with clients, my heart was changing.

I remember sitting in my favorite chair, praying, when I was prompted by the Lord to take my skills in image consulting into churches to help Christian women have more confidence in how they look. Women battle with their outer appearance, and Christian women are no different. Many times we have issues with comparison and feelings of low self-esteem. Instead of being grateful for how we are made, we berate ourselves. Struggling with the way one looks in clothes is an ever-present reality for most women. After wrestling with God over the idea of taking this message to the church, I finally did.

Over the years I've had many conversations with church leadership, explaining the benefits of confident women and how it's critical that women feel good about themselves and represent on the outside who they are on the inside. I have been privileged to walk alongside thousands of Christian women, speak at national conferences, and educate and train Christian image consultants to take the message of fashion, style, and beauty to the church to build up girls of all ages.

Kathryn Graves' *Fashioned by God* is filled with nuggets for the everyday woman. I believe that any woman who reads this and follows along with each lesson will have a heart makeover and find that she loves herself more each day. This is a serious issue for today's Christian woman, and I'm excited to recommend this book to others who may be struggling with their outer appearance and body-esteem. I'm grateful for women like Kathryn who realize that how we feel about our outer appearance is critical to our relationship with God.

Shari

Founder of Fashion Meets Faith
Author of *Help Me, Jesus, I Have Nothing to Wear!*

Introduction

When you open your closet to get dressed, do you feel overwhelmed or excited? Insecure or confident? Or do you think, *I just need to clean this thing out*?

Let me assure you, you're not alone.

Did you know your heart is like a closet? Just like an outfit you want to wear can get lost in your closet, the contents you want in your heart can be buried under other stuff.

This book is a devotional, a journal guide, and a practical wardrobe manual.

I spent many years in the fashion industry, helping women find currently fashionable outfits in their own closets. I discovered that this helped them feel better about themselves when they walked out the door in the morning. Knowing they looked good gave them a confidence boost. These same years, I also taught a weekly Bible study. Along the way, I discovered I love to write devotionals.

One day, while driving home from a writers and speakers conference, I began to consider the idea of writing something that would offer a combination of fashion tips and spiritual inspiration for the everyday woman. I stopped for a long lunch so I could write everything down. I wasn't sure about it, having never seen a book like this one before. But the Lord pressed me to write down my thoughts. My literary agent loved the idea, and you are holding the result in your hands.

My prayer for you as you read and work through *Fashioned by God* is that you will learn how to find current fashion in your closet, express your personality with your wardrobe, and clear out your closet so your choices can be easily seen. I pray you will also develop a beautiful, rewarding relationship with Jesus Christ.

Let me encourage you to make this book your jumping-off point to begin a journal with lots of space for your notes and drawings. You may find that you need more than thirty days to complete this material. Feel free to take all the time you need. There is nothing sacred about thirty days. *Fashioned by God* is really all about you. So make it yours.

Part 1

CLARIFY YOUR STYLE

Open Your Closet Doors

Examine yourselves as to whether you are in the faith.
Test yourselves. Do you not know yourselves,
that Jesus Christ is in you?
—unless indeed you are disqualified.
2 CORINTHIANS 13:5

How do you feel when you open your closet doors in the mornings? Are you afraid of what might jump out at you because of the mess? Or are you bored by items you've owned for years? Often we just don't know what to do with what we see. Our closets are filled with clothing we no longer wear because it's either too small or too big. Some items we've owned for so long, they've gone out of style. We want clothes that fit us, express our personal style, and make us look good. And we also want to honor God. But doing all of that can be challenging. When we purchase new items, there is no space in our closets for them, and we often don't know how to pair new things with what we already own.

Where do we even start? Well, the first thing we have to do to solve the problem is open the doors and look in. We've got to examine what we see hanging there.

Do you own pants in both your *big* size and your *small* size? Many of us hang on to the clothes we used to wear because we're either afraid we'll gain the weight back, or we already have and long to lose it again. Is your closet crammed with dresses that were in style ten years ago, but now they're so old, not even consignment stores want them anymore? Do you have many pairs of leggings but not much else in the pants department? Are the tops in your closet the colors you love, or ones you're not sure about? Do you own more pairs of shoes than you can count? And do you have a purse for every possible color outfit and occasion?

Before we can begin filling our closets with current high style, we need to take an honest look at what already fills them. We need to know what has to go away and what can stay. As we work through this book, we'll answer that question in detail. But for today, let's just see what we have.

Open your closet doors and take a good look inside. If items fall out on top of you, see what they are. Go all the way to the back. Consider how many of your clothes, shoes, purses, and scarves you actually wear. Is some serious clearing out in order? How do you feel about what you see in your closet? Are you willing to begin cleaning it out?

* * *

Our hearts are like closets. We sometimes don't want to look too closely at what's in them because we're afraid of what we might find. All sorts of things get stuffed in there, with each item on top of what's already there. We rarely take time to pull anything out. And even if we do, before long, it gets crammed back in. It just seems easier that way. We don't want to deal with it.

The truth is, there is really only one thing you need in your heart—one person, actually. If Jesus Christ is in there, then the other problems can be solved. Can you begin to sort through some of the mess inside your heart, making space for the one thing you really need? Consider today what might be worth pulling out, sorting through, and maybe even letting go.

Lord Jesus, I confess that I have neglected to clean out my cluttered mind and heart. What I see in there scares me sometimes. I need you to help me re-organize my life and priorities. I'm asking you to show me what needs to go and what can stay. Thank you for loving me enough to provide this help.

Heart Action

- Examine your mind. What's stored in there? Go all the way to the back. Is Jesus Christ inside? Is he covered over with clutter? How do you feel about what you see in your heart? In the space below, list a few things God said to you after you prayed.

- List the obvious things you need to take out.

- If you're not sure Jesus is in your heart, read these verses: Romans 3:23; Romans 6:23; John 3:3; John 14:6; Romans 10:9–11; 2 Corinthians 5:15; and Revelation 3:20.

Wardrobe Action

The beauty of a woman must be seen from her eyes, because that is the doorway to her heart, the place where love resides.
—Audrey Hepburn

- Consider your pairs of pants. Do you own multiple sizes?

- Sort through the dresses and skirts. Assess each for current style potential. Make a list of the sizes and how many you are absolutely certain you will never wear again.

- Pull out your tops and blouses. Don't feel bad if there are lots of them. Think about the colors in each one. Do you love them? Check out the fit. Is this a top you love to wear? If not, ask yourself why.

- Count your pairs of shoes and purses. This may seem painful, as it requires facing up to the real number. Also count scarves.

- Open your lingerie drawer. Does what you see scare you? Is it a disaster of disorganization, filled with one too many tattered and torn items? Consider if it may be time to clean out this space.

- For today, you can put most items back in your closet. There may be a few things that you instinctively know you need to leave out, and that's great. Now is a good time to find a spot where you can store them while you complete your closet clean-out.

- If you're stressed about all the things that need to go, don't worry. We'll talk on Day 6 about what to do with old clothes after you clear them out. Some may simply be headed for the trash can, but for most items, you'll have a variety of options.

Foundation Repair

*For no other foundation can anyone lay
than that which is laid, which is Jesus Christ.*

1 CORINTHIANS 3:11

*He is like a man building a house, who dug deep and laid the
foundation on the rock. And when the flood arose, the stream
beat vehemently against that house, and could not shake it,
for it was founded on the rock.*

LUKE 6:48

We need to begin with first things first. Without the proper foundations, no clothing will look good on us or even fit well. And that means starting with the basics—lingerie.

When you opened your lingerie drawer yesterday, did you find a tangled mess? Did you need to press down with one hand and shove the drawer closed with the other just to make it all fit? If you own a lingerie chest with smaller-size drawers, each category of items will go in a separate drawer. If you own a dresser or chest of drawers, your larger drawers can house multiple types. Let's see what sorts of things belong in these drawers and how to make them beautiful spaces.

We'll begin with panties. These need to have great function, comfort, and style. One very important thing to consider is that they need to be constructed so no lines appear under pants or skirts. Try several different types to find your preference. Always check your backside in a mirror before going out.

Next, let's talk about bras, our foundational support. The shoulder straps should be comfortable and hide under your clothes. It might be a fad now to allow contrast color bra straps to show, but consider the image you want to portray. Coco Chanel said, "A girl should be two things: classy and fabulous." Good bras are an investment that needs to last through fads. Because of the need to hide under clothes, you may need one or two racer-back-style bras. Make this decision based on the shoulder cuts of your summer tops and dresses.

The number of bras you own is a personal decision, but it needs to be enough that you allow a day in between wearings for the elastic to rest. And enough so you only need to launder them once a week. Unless you're doing sweaty work, you can wear a bra two or three times before washing.

When was the last time you bought new undergarments? If you can't even remember, it might be a good time to schedule a shopping trip. Buying these items is stressful for me, so I try to allow a couple of hours and go alone. After I make my purchases, I go to a coffee shop to help myself unwind.

What do you sleep in? Would you describe it as pretty or merely functional? Or worse, is it raggedy? Sleepwear doesn't have to be sexy to be pretty. But if you're married, a bit of sexy in the lingerie drawer is fantastic. Sleepwear deserves its own large drawer, if you can manage it. In a lingerie chest, you may want to divide sleepwear into more than a single drawer.

Do you keep socks and hosiery in the same drawer as sleepwear and foundations? If so, you might want to rethink that arrangement. If you can designate a drawer for socks and hosiery, all the better. Do you have to rummage for matches to your socks? Do your tights end up twisted with your bras? Too many different kinds of clothing stored in one place can make it impossible to tell what is really there and make finding the right item in the morning a real challenge.

* * *

Have you checked your spiritual foundations lately? Have you allowed disorganization or clutter to overtake your daily routines? Is your regular Bible reading so ripped and torn, you've about given up on it? Consider today what your spiritual foundation looks like, and whether it is in need of repair the way your lingerie drawer might be. Don't let the thought overwhelm you; instead, start at the beginning.

Does your faith rest on Jesus Christ? Any other foundation will shift and slide. Religious activity is good, but is only valuable when it is an expression of our faith and not what we build our faith upon.

We need a daily conversation with the Lord to keep our lives fresh and clean and orderly. When we read the Bible, we are listening to him speak. When we pray, we are talking to him. These are the two aspects of conversation—and we need them both to maintain a relationship. Do you worship with other believers on a regular basis? If it's been a while since you went to church, maybe it's time to return. The fellowship of like-minded individuals can refresh your soul and help keep your foundations strong.

Father, I realize I have let my personal Bible reading and prayer time lapse. Because I'm not as familiar with the Bible as I should be, I've become open to some ideas that may not be true. Help me re-establish my spiritual disciplines in order to repair my foundation. Thank you that I know I can take it all the way back to Jesus Christ and rebuild from there.

- What time of day works best for you to read your Bible and pray?
- Put your daily quiet time on your calendar.
- What changes might you need to make to fit it in? What might you need to eliminate?
- Is weekly worship with others on your calendar? If not, consider adding it today.

Wardrobe Action

Delete the negative. Accentuate the positive!
—Donna Karan

- If you find any torn or worn-out foundations or sleepwear in your drawer(s), remove them. These will become trash. Find a trash bag, place the items in it, close it up, and take it out right away. You don't want to be tempted to keep anything ragged, no matter how much you may love it.
- Eliminate any tights with snags and socks without mates.
- Check for bras that allow no longer hold their shape. You can wait until you've replaced them to throw them away. Count how many new ones you need to purchase based on the guidelines above.
- Sort through panties. If you already know certain ones cause lines, toss them. Otherwise, make sure to check each time you dress. As you discover ones

that need to go away, don't hesitate. Now that you are aware, it will be easy to get rid of them.

- If you need to buy new panties, make a note of how many.

- If your sleepwear situation left you with nothing, today might be a good time to plan a shopping trip.

- Breathe. This might be the most difficult part of stylish dressing. The worst is over now!

DAY 3

Pants Parade

*I will instruct you and teach you in the way you should go;
I will guide you with My eye.*

PSALM 32:8

How many pairs of pants did you find in your closet the other day? Most women I know own far more pairs than they wear. These days, pants are an integral part of most outfits. They can be worn to work, school, and even funerals and weddings. Of course, the occasion determines the level of dressiness. Leggings have even made the transition from athletic wear to daily wear. The question becomes, what type of pants go with what type of occasion? And how many pairs do you really need? Here are some guidelines to help you sort through the various categories of pants you ought to keep in your closet.

Straight leg or bootcut knit dress pants go with blouses, silky tops, and pretty jackets or sweaters. These are suitable for the office or anywhere you want to project a professional image. I recommend one pair each in black, gray, and navy. A white pair can also be nice. Fashion designers try to add an unexpected touch each season, and as I write this, white is trending for fall. So if you like white, you're in luck, because it may be here to stay year-round.

Ankle pants can be worn to the office if they are suit material with a sharp crease down the front. These can also be paired with a blouse or knit top and a jacket. The same advice for number and color as straight leg or bootcut dress pants applies here.

Skinny knit pants (not leggings) go under longer tops. These can be dressy, but not for the office unless it's a more casual setting. This combo is also great for a night out. Women with apple-shaped or pear-shaped bodies can choose this look with confidence because it covers their *fluffy* parts and highlights their thinner legs. It is nice to have at least a couple pairs of these pants, say one navy and one black.

Leggings can go under a short, belted shirtdress and be worn with high heels for an office-appropriate look. As a general rule though, leggings are not pants. They should be treated more like tights. They should never be worn under a top that does not cover the entire front and back of the torso. Use your full-length mirror to ensure this. Ideally, the top will end at or just below mid-thigh. Also, leggings should be of sufficient weight not to be sheer. If you're self-conscious about your legs or don't enjoy showing off your thighs, you might want to pass on leggings unless your top ends at your knees. If you do wear them, you may want to have a black pair, a denim-look pair, and possibly a white pair.

Athletic wear might be current fashion for daywear, but not at the office. Wear a casual, athletic look for athletic events, vacations, or time spent at home. Beware of shopping for new clothes while wearing athletic wear. Sneakers and a pair of dress pants just look weird in the dressing room mirror, not to mention you can't judge the length if you intend to wear the pants with heels.

Capri pants are, in my view, an unfortunate version of pants. They end at the widest part of the calf and emphasize it. Wide-leg capris are also a no. (Sometimes these are called gauchos.) If shorter pants are desired, an ankle pant is much more flattering and can be found in casual fabrics and styles. If shorts are desired, longer Bermuda shorts cover everything except the knee. I advise taking capris out of your closet. The caveat to this advice is for tall, willowy women. If you want your calves to appear larger or your legs to appear shorter, capris just might be for you.

Jeans have become ubiquitous. Even casual jeans can be dressed up with a top, jacket, or sweater. In most cases, jeans are not appropriate for office wear except possibly on a casual Friday, but they are a go-to for almost every casual occasion. They come in every style, cut, and length. I own shorter skinny jeans, longer bootcut jeans, full-flare dressy jeans, dark denim, light and even white denim, and some bright colors. It is fun to be creative with denim style! The thing to keep in mind is your body type. If you're short like me, a longer leg worn with stacked heels gives the illusion of height. If you're tall, you can emphasize your long legs or wear skinny jeans with flats to appear shorter. I recommend one pair in each of your favorite styles.

Now a word about *muffin tops*. Women who try to wear a waistband smaller than their actual waist end up looking bigger than they are. This is the muffin-top effect. Those of us with a loose middle can struggle with this effect. So it may be a good idea to wear a fuller-cut top to help camouflage the pouf. I'm not talking about a muumuu here. A tailored top in the right size can flow over bulges.

No matter how many pairs of pants you keep in your closet, make sure each has a purpose in your life and can be worn with both comfort and style.

* * *

We have focused on choosing the appropriate pants in cut, style, fabric, and fit for the occasion and your body shape. Did you know we wear spiritual *pants* too? These are the basics of our spiritual wardrobe—the workhorses, what pulls all the rest together. And they keep us together around the middle. I'm talking about our basic routines. Praying, attending church, Bible reading, and journaling, for example. We all need to do these things. But the form they take and the time we spend on each is personal—our body type, if you will. Some of us can spend more time than others reading our Bibles because of our stage of life or occupation. Some of us need to journal our prayers. Some of us prefer to pray while out for a jog. My husband prays at each red light while he's driving. Some of us attend church on Sunday and some on Saturday. Some of us prefer in-depth daily Bible study, while others carry a purse-size devotional book.

The point is not the style of your *pants*, but that you wear them. We don't even want to think what an outfit might look like if a woman forgot her pants! Just so, your spiritual life needs *pants*. Spend some time considering what works best for you in each area. What is your preferred spiritual pants style?

Father, thank you that you made me just the way I am. You gave me the preference for my personal style. Please instruct me as I consider how best to express my style in worshiping you.

Heart Action

- Did you already put a daily Bible reading and prayer time on your calendar?

- Do you prefer a study or a devotional?

- Do you have a devotional or study you're currently using, or do you need to find a new one for this season?

- Did you add weekly worship attendance to your calendar yesterday? If not, put it on your schedule now. If you need to find a church, go online and check out church websites. Ask friends for references. Read the doctrinal statements of churches that interest you. Do they match your own beliefs?

- Do you pray best with a journal or not? If you've never tried journaling, find one with some question prompts (such as this book).

Wardrobe Action

Fashion is what you're offered four times a year by designers.
And style is what you choose.
—Lauren Hutton

- Take out of your closet every pair of pants that is not the size you currently wear.

- Of the ones left in your closet, check each for fit. Are they comfortable? Do you like the color? Do they wear well? (As in, do they wrinkle at the crotch or ride up in the wrong places?) Do they flatter your figure? Do you like how they look?

- If the answer is no to any of the above questions, don't keep them. Put the discards in the pile of clothes you are storing until you choose the best home for each. I will help you figure that out on Day 6.

- Have you worn them in the last year? If not, why not? Do you really need to keep them if you don't wear them? Try to keep only what you love and wear.

- If you feel overwhelmed, start with out-of-season pants. Then work your way through current-season pairs.

- Did you keep at least one in every category? (Skinny, bootcut, straight leg, ankle, shorts, suit material, denim, knit, etc.) If not, was it because you feel you don't look your best in a certain style, or because you don't own a pair in that style after cleaning out?

- Did you notice a color you are missing in the keeper group?

- Make a list of new pants you need to purchase if something seems to be lacking.

DAY 4

Topsy Turvy

But the fruit of the Spirit is love, joy, peace, longsuffering,
kindness, goodness, faithfulness, gentleness, self-control.
Against such there is no law.
GALATIANS 5:22–23

Tops are one of the pretty parts of our wardrobe. They can also be a bit tricky to get right. I need tops with a bit of tailoring to keep me from looking like a snow woman. You know, a big ball for the legs and feet, a big ball for the torso, and, well, we'll leave it there.

So let's consider the shape of top you might look best in. I have a smallish waist, but because I'm short-waisted and short in stature, my tops need seams to show it off. I have a client who needs box-shaped tops because she has an apple figure. A long, straight top helps offset the roundness of her middle. Another client is tall and willowy. She looks great in gathered, flowing tops that give her the illusion of more substance. Take a look at yourself in the mirror. What shape are you? Keep this in mind later today when we take some action steps.

Along with shape, the neckline of a top can make a

big difference in how it looks on you. Because I have broader shoulders, a V-neck top is the most flattering. I can wear round necklines as well; however, a boatneck only emphasizes my wide shoulders.

How do you know which neckline is best for you? V-neck tops will soften fullness at the jaw, chin, or neck, and show off the collar bones. A round neck draws the eye toward the chin and neck. A sweetheart neckline softens and flatters most shapes. And as we've discussed, a boatneck will accent and visually broaden the shoulders. Go back to the mirror and think about which features you want to emphasize and which you might like to minimize. Then choose tops to achieve that goal with the most flattering necklines.

Another issue to consider in the shape category is cleavage. Some seasons this is more of an issue than others when shopping. A few years ago, it was almost impossible to find tops cut high enough for my personal taste. The main point is just to be mindful of the cleavage when considering a neckline.

Color is what often draws us to a particular top. What are your favorite colors? Do the tops in your closet reflect these? What colors look best near your face? An easy way to tell is to put on a pure white blouse. Then put on a creamy off-white one. Which makes you look more alive and upbeat? If the white one does, you need to stick with cool colors around your face. If the creamy one does, wear more warm colors. How do you know which is cool and which is warm? If there is a yellow base to the color, it is warm. If there is a blue base to the color, it is cool. You can wear every color, just not every shade of every color.

I need warm colors. This means I can wear chartreuse green, but not mid-summer grass green. I can wear orange-red but not blue-red. I can wear strawberry pink, but not fuchsia. If you aren't sure what flatters you most, invite a friend over and play in your closet. Sometimes all it takes is a second opinion to confirm your instincts.

Did you know you can use color to make yourself look taller or shorter? Even thinner? Color breaks are one way to do this. A color break is when the color changes. For instance, a white top over black pants with a red belt gives the appearance of three separate color areas. The more of these you wear, the shorter you will appear. And the place on your body where the break happens is the part accented. For many women, it helps if color breaks happen at our thinnest parts.

Stripes are another aid in this area. Horizontal stripes make us appear wider and vertical stripes make us look taller and thinner. Maybe you want to accent your trim arms. You might like a solid top with striped sleeves. Or if you are tall, you might like several wide bands of different colors on a top. If your bust is small, choosing a wide, horizontal stripe in that area can help you look fuller. Conversely, if it is larger, a vertical center stripe can minimize it.

A large pattern can make the eye travel in a meandering way, while a mini print can make the eye take shorter turns. Plaids work in the same way, with large plaids causing the eye to look across and up and down. So if a top has a pattern in the fabric, check to be sure it leads the viewer's eye where you want it to go.

What sorts of tops reside in your closet? Are they mostly T-shirts? Or are you like another client of mine? She says she likes a casual look, but every time she buys a top, she realizes later it is dressy; she doesn't gravitate to casual wear in the store. We need to be comfortable with our personal style.

My friend is not a T-shirt and jeans gal, and she knows it. She just would like to add a few for at-home days. On the flip side, some of my friends own more T-shirts than any other style top. What is your style?

＊＊＊

What is the pretty, colorful part of our spiritual lives? It is the part others see first that impacts them. Our behavior, born from our attitude, is the first thing others notice about us. What we say and do indicates what is inside of us. If our foundations are in good shape, then we will begin to wear beautiful behaviors, attracting attention for all the right reasons. Galatians 5:22–23 tells us what these beautiful attitudes and behaviors consist of. Do you exhibit these *colors* each day? Are you wearing the fruits of the Spirit, or are you too often bogged down in drab, dark, or messy outer layers that prevent the love of Christ from shining through? Consider how you might allow your spiritual colors to shine more clearly, attracting others and allowing them to catch a glimpse of God working through you.

Heavenly Father, I want to wear beautiful behavior and be attractive in your eyes. Help me remember what that looks like, even when things are tough. Keep my eyes open to the truth.

Heart Action

- Write or draw pictures of your personal definition of each of the fruits listed in Galatians 5:22–23.

- Color them.

- Do any of these fruits look a bit shriveled in your life? If so, list those and ask the Lord to help you cultivate them.

- What are a few things you could do to cultivate the less robust fruits?

Wardrobe Action

Attitude is everything.
—Diane von Furstenberg

- Pull every top, sweater, and jacket out of your closet. (This includes tanks and camisoles.)

- Sort for sizes. Keep only the size you wear right now. Holding on to what used to fit, or what you hope might fit again, only clutters your closet.

- Don't worry if you're overwhelmed by the number. Marie Kondo, author of *The Life-Changing Magic of Tidying Up*, says the average number of tops in a woman's closet is 160! Start with out-of-season tops to make it easier.

- Go through the keep pile and pull out any colors you either don't like or that don't flatter you.

Dress-querade

I will sing for joy in God, explode in praise from deep in my soul! He dressed me up in a suit of salvation, he outfitted me in a robe of righteousness, as a bridegroom who puts on a tuxedo and a bride a jeweled tiara.

ISAIAH 61:10–11 MSG

My mother's cedar chest is half full of period dresses handed down from our ancestors. My own cedar chest holds the wedding gown both my mother and I wore.

Old clothes can be precious. Or they can just be plain old. Other than heirloom items, out-of-style dresses tend to congregate in the back of our closets. We loved them once upon a time. We remember looking and feeling great when we wore them. Unable to part with them, we hung them in the back. Though we can't see them, we are comforted knowing they are there.

Is a section of your closet occupied by dresses like this? What is a woman to do with them? How do we know a dress needs to move to the back rather than grouping it with current wearables?

This book is more about style than fashion. That means

we are focusing on items that stand the test of time and will always look good with the addition of accessories, or combined in fresh ways with other pieces. Keeping this in mind, follow these tips to help sort through your dresses today.

First, determine what is the best dress length (or two) for you. Tall women can wear mid-calf length, but shorter women need hemlines at or just above or below the kneecap. If you are one of the lucky ones with beautiful, long legs and a long torso to match, a shorter skirt/dress length can look fabulous, within reason. Just below mid-thigh is the shortest length that I feel comfortable and modest in; but if that is too short for you, keep it longer. Remember that very short dresses are for evening wear or athletic wear only. You should keep the occasion in mind. Office attire requires hemlines at the knee or longer. And anyone can look amazing in a floor-length dress for a formal occasion or a maxi dress for casual occasions.

Second, consider style. If a dress is older than three or four years, it probably will be out of style. An exception to this rule is a straight, black, knee-length, sleeveless dress. It can be changed with jewelry or a scarf, sweater, jacket, or belt. I own one I bought ten years ago, and I still wear it often. I just change it up with accessories.

Current hemline fads can change every season. But if you own only what flatters your legs, you'll always be in style. This is why I'm a big fan of knee-length dresses and skirts. They always seem to look stylish, and every woman looks great in them.

Another consideration when it comes to style is the neckline. The neckline on a dress can shift it from daywear to evening wear. Any revealing cut must be reserved for evenings. The wrap dress is a favorite day dress for many, with good reason. It makes the most of your shape, nipping in the waist and accenting the bust line without revealing it. However, if the V of the neckline plunges too far, larger-busted women should avoid them. And if the fabric is clingy, apple-shaped women might want to opt out, as it may accentuate bulges.

Gathered skirts will accent our hips, but can also give the illusion of a small waist. No matter our size, this can be a dynamic look, especially with the addition of a belt. The only caution I would give is to women shaped like me. I'm not overweight, but my bust line is relatively large for my short height. If I wear gathered skirts, I look like a round snowball.

Know yourself and go with what you like to see in the mirror.

The cut of a dress also determines its style quotient. Certain cuts come and go from fashion, like suit jackets with shoulder pads over long pencil skirts. Large shoulder pads in anything—top, dress, or jacket—can date the item. You'll learn later in this book how to know what is current, but one thing that helps is just to look around. If nobody else is wearing big shoulder pads (or any other style you might be wondering about), you might want to consider letting go of yours.

Color is another important consideration. Use the same guidelines for dresses as for tops. Also, color and pattern can determine whether a dress is current. Some years geometrics reign, other years, solids or florals, and some years, anything goes. Again, look around you.

We've just come through a long phase when pants ruled over dresses. But as I write this, dresses are making a big comeback. If you like the pretty, feminine look of dresses, wear them!

* * *

Did you know the Lord gives us a dress? Jesus Christ died, was buried, and rose again to give us eternal life. When we accept this life, he dresses us with his righteousness. Our old, ugly dresses of sin are gone.

Imagine exchanging your old, ugly dress that came handed down to you for a brand-new, beautiful white ball gown with glittering sparkles all over it. The old one didn't even fit properly, because it wasn't made for you. The new one is tailor made for you and accents your beauty.

That's what really happens to our hearts when Jesus comes in. Our old clothes, stained by the ashes of sin, are whisked away. Psalm 30:11–12 tells us, "You have turned for me my mourning into dancing; you have put off my sackcloth and clothed me with gladness, to the end that my glory may sing praise to You and not be silent. O Lord my God, I will give thanks to You forever!"

Do you remember how you felt when you wore your first prom dress, or your wedding dress? If you have a dress from a special occasion in the back of your closet, do you remember how you felt the day you wore it?

This is the same feeling we have when we get our new *dress* of righteousness from God. How can we keep silent about such a marvelous thing? When we talk about the *dresses* the Lord gives us, and how we feel when we wear them, praises come to mind. The rest of our spiritual being is draped in praise when we realize what he has done for us.

Lord Jesus, thank you for taking my sins on the cross. Thank you for loving me enough to die for me. You alone are worthy of all praise and glory! You have dressed me up in the most beautiful dress of righteousness and put a tiara of joy on my head. I love you, Lord.

- If you're married, do you remember how beautiful you felt on your wedding day? (If not, don't you know how beautiful all brides are?) In the same way, relish the beauty of the *dress* of righteousness given to you. You are the bride of Christ.

Wardrobe Action

*The older I get, and the more collections I do,
the more I'm driven by real style and beauty.*
—Phoebe Philo

- Pull all the dresses and skirts out of your closet. Check all the closets in the house for random dress-hiding spots. Lay them all on your bed.

- Put aside any items that are not in your current size.

- If a dress is more than three years old, evaluate it for style. You can keep it, but you may need to pair it in a fresh way with a scarf or belt that will bring it up to date. I'll teach you how to do this later in the book.

- Is the color a good one for you? Is the cut flattering to your figure? If not, put it aside.

- Is this an heirloom? (Did you wear it to prom, or to your graduation or another memorable event?) If the answer is yes, do you have a place to store it? Do you need to have it professionally preserved? You may be able to keep these, but only if you can find an appropriate storage spot.

What to Do with All This Stuff?

As far as the east is from the west,
so far has He removed our transgressions from us.

PSALM 103:12

Along about now, you may be wondering what to do with all the clothes you don't want to put back into your closet. Some are perfectly good, some are in good condition but out of date, and some are just plain ratty. You have several options. But let's process each so we can make sure the destination of each item is appropriate for it.

Consignment shops are perfect for any clothing in current style and pristine condition. This might be the place for items in a wrong size that you hardly ever wore. Or maybe now you realize some colors or cuts are just wrong for you, but the item is almost new. The thought of getting at least some financial return eases the pain of parting with good clothes.

Thrift shops and benevolence closets love to receive clothing in good condition, even if it might be slightly out of date. This is the best choice for items three or four years old, especially if they have a tiny flaw—*tiny* being the key word. Nobody wants to wear clothes with big snags or obvious holes, even if they are free or cost very little.

Ministries like Dress for Success give office-appropriate clothing to women trying to get back on their feet after a rough patch in their lives. Most of the time, the outfits are worn for job interviews. These places want current fashion less than three years old.

You may opt for selling clothing at a garage sale. In my area, larger sizes tend to sell best, along with children's clothing. If you already plan to host a sale in the near future, and your clothes fit the target market in your area, this may work for you. But be advised, it works best if you have many other items for sale as well. Another great option might be selling clothing online.

Trash is the last resort, unless the items are intimate apparel. In that case, it is the first resort. Nobody wants to buy or even be given this type of used item. Trash is also the spot for torn, snagged items; things with holes (that aren't supposed to be there!); obviously worn-out pieces, seriously old and outdated clothes; and anything you would not want to be given for free if you were on the receiving end.

Having made these distinctions, it will be easier to part with all the extra clothes you no longer need.

* * *

We all have things in our lives we know don't need to be there. Words spoken that we regret, anger flare-ups, behaviors we're not proud of—on and on the list goes. As we examine our lives the way we are our clothes, we realize the need to cast off much more than we ever thought. How do we get rid of these things? Jesus tells us that if we confess our sins, he is faithful to forgive us our sins and cleanse us from all unrighteousness (1 John 1:9). Once we become aware of what we need to stop doing or thinking, or that we've neglected to do or say, it is time to confess it. That means agreeing with God's view of it. Then we take it out.

What does it look like to get rid of our sin? Once we agree with God about it, we need to repent from it. Turn away from it. Change our actions and attitudes about it. Jesus will take away the penalty of the sin. The trash is the only option for sin. But we still might need to apologize to someone or make restitution. We might need to begin including somebody we've previously ignored in our social group. If your sin involved another person, ask the Lord what you need to do to make things right with them.

It's hard to be so brutally honest with ourselves. Most of the time, I am the last person to become aware of my sins. I tend to rationalize my words and actions in a way that makes them seem not so bad to myself. It's painful to admit how wrong I am. But it's necessary. None of us need to keep behaviors and words in our lives that do not reflect our best.

Once we recognize and confess our sins, we can leave them with God and trust him to take it to his trash.

Lord Jesus, I confess. I realize that my attitude about some things in my life has not been the same as yours. I need your forgiveness. I agree with you and ask you to take away my sins and help me gain your perspective. I don't want to do, say, or think these things anymore. Thank you for your grace in these matters.

Heart Action

- Make a list of what you need to confess.

- Pray over your list.

- Use a permanent marker to cross out those items after you pray.

- Create designs over and around your crossed-out words. See if you can make a pleasant, colorful picture.

- Consider whether there are any action steps you need to take in order to make things right with another person.

Wardrobe Action

Elegance is elimination.
—Cristobal Balenciaga

- Go to the storage pile of clothes you have taken out of your closet.

- Sort items by their appropriate destination, as indicated in today's reading.

- Bag up the items and label the bags with the destination intended for the contents. Put them in your vehicle, ready for transport. Take trash bags out now.

- How do you feel now that these things are out and appropriately dealt with? Do you feel lighter? Happier? Excited?

- If you have time, begin transporting your bags to the places you've chosen today.

Shoe Market

You will show me the path of life;
In Your presence is fullness of joy;
At Your right hand are pleasures forevermore.
PSALM 16:11

And all the people went up after him;
and the people played the flutes and rejoiced with great joy,
so that the earth seemed to split with their sound.
1 KINGS 1:40

Do you own so many pairs of shoes that you might be able to open a shoe store? There is nothing wrong with a shoe habit, as long as your budget can support it. However, we need to make sure the shoes we store in our closets are shoes we wear. They need to be the perfect addition to an outfit, enable us to exercise in comfort, or make us feel glamorous. A function of some kind is important. If we own pairs of shoes whose only purpose is taking up valuable real estate in our closets, they need to go.

In this chapter, we'll discuss dressy shoes and heels. Tomorrow we'll talk about other kinds of shoes.

It took me a lot of years to comprehend the importance of shoes to an outfit. When I entered the fashion industry, my shoes were mostly inexpensive, utility shoes. Not that price makes the shoe—but I only shopped for basic shoes, and I wore the same brown or black loafer all winter and the same white or black sandal all summer. The only thought I gave to coordinating shoes with clothes was whether I should wear the black ones or brown ones.

My peers at Premier Designs pointed this out to me and taught me that shoes may be the most important part of an outfit—next to accessories. They certainly can take an ensemble from ho-hum to *wow*!

A case in point is my black patent leather Mary Jane pumps with three-inch chunky heels. When I wear them with ankle pants, the effect is dynamite. Flat sandals would work, but not add pizzazz.

Color also makes all the difference. Imagine green ankle pants with white sandals. Now imagine the same pants with red heels. I can see a light bulb turning on in your head!

So which shoes really take an outfit to the next level?

High heels help make us appear taller and thinner. I would venture to guess that most women reading this find that appealing. If you think you can't wear heels, stay tuned. Tomorrow we'll discuss fit and orthotics.

Of course, no matter how well the shoe is built, some cannot wear heels for medical reasons. But perhaps you could wear a platform shoe. These can give height without raising the heel above alignment with the toes.

If you are tall, don't be afraid of heels. One of my clients is six feet tall, but she wears heels sometimes, just because she loves them. What's another few inches at that height? My daughter-in-law is taller than my son. But she doesn't let that deter her love of heels. They both are comfortable with her height. It doesn't hurt that she carries herself with grace since she's a ballerina.

As with any other category of apparel, shoes express our personal style. But shoes can add the extra punch. We can be a bit more adventurous with shoes than clothes for office wear. If you work in a place where your clothing options are limited, express yourself with shoes. As I mentioned above, even black shoes, styled right, can make an impact.

* * *

Does your spiritual life seem bland or boring? Do you opt for function over form?

Just like God created a colorful, interesting planet for us to live on, he desires us to live in a vibrant relationship with him. There is nothing boring about God. In the New Testament, where the Holy Spirit's power is mentioned, the Greek word is *dunamis* (Acts 1:8). This is where we get our English word *dynamite*. Let your devotional life become an adventure as you discover new truths, dive into new territory, and snuggle under the comfort of God's love. If you feel like you've been stuck in a rut, try something new in your spiritual life. Switch up your readings, try a different location, move outside, or incorporate dance or art—find new ways to connect with God that allow you to enjoy different aspects of his creation. As you take creative risks, you'll find that God wants to take you deeper and show you more of himself.

Oh Lord, I want to experience incredible joy in your presence. I long for beauty and variety in my relationship with you. Show me gems and treasures as I read my Bible today. Make me more aware of you in every area of my life.

Heart Action

- Does your personal Bible study consist of reading random verses? Choose a book of the Bible to read through, and set a goal to read one chapter each day.

- After reading, ask what the theme of the chapter is.

- Ask what God is saying to you in this chapter.

- Write or draw the answer.

Wardrobe Action

*I firmly believe that with the right footwear
one can rule the world.*
—Bette Midler

- Sort the shoes in your closet into two groups—heels and dressy shoes, and all other shoes.

- Are there dull, boring, utilitarian shoes in your dressy pile? Pare them down by keeping only the prettiest, the most striking, and the ones in the best condition.

- Are there any daring shoes in your dressy pile?

- Do you need to buy a few new pairs with heels or in different colors to spice up your wardrobe?

- Consider the condition of those you choose not to keep. Sort the same way you did other clothes.

DAY 8

Shoe Market—
Part Two

*No longer do I call you servants, for a servant does not know
what his master is doing; but I have called you friends, for all
things that I heard from My Father I have made known to you.*

JOHN 15:15

You've taken stock of your dress shoe situation. Now you
need to go a step further (pun intended). How many of your
shoes actually feel good on your feet?

You might think high heels aren't supposed to be
comfortable. While they are not designed only for comfort,
they should not hurt your feet as soon as you slip them on.
A good-quality high heel will be constructed with a toe box
wide enough for your foot and in such a way that your foot
does not slide forward, pinching your toes.

We also need to consider the particular needs of
our own feet. Some of us have bunions, which necessitate
a wider toe box. Some have arch troubles and need extra
arch support. Some struggle with bone spurs and love to
find shoes made with memory foam insoles. Then there are

50

those among us with narrow feet or heels. These are only some of the issues facing us when trying on a pair of shoes. The good thing is that manufacturers have noticed. It is now possible to buy super-cute shoes with built-in help for problem feet.

Another focus we need to keep in mind is function. If a shoe is designed more for looks, don't try to go for a jog—even to catch a bus. If a shoe is designed for running, you probably don't want to wear it to the office. Nurses and other professionals whose jobs require them to stand or walk most of the day (or night) have discovered a few brands that cater to their needs. Ballet flats might be fun and cute, but remember they are designed, despite the name, for more sitting time and less standing or walking time. Ballerinas are trained in how to take proper steps, and even *they* dance in special toe shoes.

Concerning fit, it is best not to cram your foot into a too-tight shoe just because the store doesn't carry your size in that shoe, or because you think your foot is too big, or any other reason. Taking care of your feet in younger years ensures the ability to wear a wider variety of shoes longer in life.

Does this information change the way you view your shoes? Maybe you need to take a second look and sort through them again with comfort, function, and fit in mind. Weed out the ones that don't meet your standards in each of these areas.

Life is too short to cram our feet into shoes that don't work for us.

It's important for our shoes, and all our clothes for that matter, to be comfortable to wear. If not, don't we avoid them, pushing them aside for *special* occasions? We need to ask ourselves the comfort question about our relationship with God too. We surely don't want to avoid him or push him aside for any reason—but sometimes it happens, even with me.

How comfortable are you with God? Is he like a friend, or more like a distant relative? Does he seem like a real father, or does that idea scare you? If your relationship with your father wasn't pleasant, or worse, it may be difficult to envision the positives of God as your father.

I never felt good enough for my father. He talked openly about how he was disappointed when I was born a girl instead of a boy. He tried to make me like sports, but I'm not at all coordinated and don't even like to fish. When I reached my teen years, other dynamics in our family led me to believe I was just extra baggage for my dad. Ultimately, we discovered he had betrayed us all with a long series of extra-marital affairs going back years. For this reason, I struggled to believe God could love me. I thought I wasn't good enough. I can't even explain the weight that lifted when I realized I didn't have to be good enough—that God loved me just because. Period.

We need to set aside memories of imperfect earthly fathers. Instead, we must remind ourselves that God is the perfect father, the epitome of everything a father should be.

In addition to seeing God as a father, remember that Jesus also called us his friends. Do you have a BFF? I'm fortunate to have more than one. Isn't it wonderful to be able to tell her anything and everything and know she understands, that she always has your back? Girlfriends are a special gift to us. They support us when our world is crashing down around us. They are fun to be around and enjoy the same things we do. Some are more adventurous than we are. They lead us out of our comfort zones into all kinds of crazy antics and special, meaningful moments.

Let God the Father and Jesus the Friend into your life. The rich experiences you'll gain will be worth whatever it costs you in courage. Really open up to the Lord. Let him begin to smooth the hurts and light up your darkest days. You can tell him anything. He'll understand. And he always has your back.

Lord, thank you for loving me like a father and a friend. I love you too, and want our relationship to reflect this. Help me learn to talk to you and listen to your words as I read them in the Bible. Make me more aware of your presence.

Heart Action

- Read Proverbs 12:26; 17:17; 18:24; and 27:9 to discover some qualities of a good friend.
- List some of your friends who come to mind when you read these verses.
- Are you a good friend to others?
- Do you view friendship with Jesus a little differently now?
- What can you do to become a closer friend of Jesus?
- What concepts of God as father do you need to let go of? Can you run to him with every need or problem you face? List the ones you need to talk to him about today.

Wardrobe Action

The most courageous act is still to think for yourself. Aloud.
—Coco Chanel

- Go through your shoe collection again, with comfort, function, and fit in mind.
- How many pairs fail these three tests?
- Can you part with the shoes that fail?

Purse Palooza

*But you shall appoint the Levites over the tabernacle of the
Testimony, over all its furnishings, and over all things that
belong to it; they shall carry the tabernacle and
all its furnishings; they shall attend to it and camp
around the tabernacle.*

NUMBERS 1:50

Just about the time I think I've found the perfect purse, I see a different one in a store that is to die for. I'm relatively new to the love of purses, as I am to shoes. But I am smitten. I used to be the one with a functional brown shoulder bag big enough to carry anything I might possibly ever need. And I carried it everywhere, with every outfit. Now, however, I'm more in tune with color coordination and size to suit function.

When going out to dinner, a wristlet will do. But for a trip, my oversized duffel or backpack comes along. Styles change for purses from season to season, just like for clothes. Sometimes large purses reign. Sometimes a structured bag is in, and the next thing I know, a cross-body drawstring bag is all the rage. At this writing, circle-shaped, structured shoulder bags can be seen in style shows.

Like shoes, purses are an easy way to add bling and color to an outfit. The nice thing about purses is that they don't need to fit our feet. We can carry whatever kind of bag suits our personal preference at any given moment.

My mother saved some of my grandmother's old purses. One is a silver- and pearl-beaded evening bag with a long silver chain. It even has beaded fringe on the bottom. Another is a small black leather coin purse with a ball-snap closure. I remember seeing Grandma carry this little gem when we rode the bus in the city. She kept her tokens inside it. But I do not remember the evening bag. If my mother had not saved it, I'd never have known this side of my grandmother.

Purses say a lot about our style and the things we like to do. One of my daughters-in-law is an athlete. She carries a backpack much of her leisure time. And she prefers simplicity. So for work, she keeps it simple with a black computer purse. The other of my girls loves purses and color. I never know, when I see her, which purse she'll be carrying. She is also a businesswoman, but she still manages to express her colorful style with purses.

This is an area where budget and storage space will determine as much as personal preferences. We will discuss budgets and storage later. For now, enjoy expressing your style with purses, with one caveat. If you no longer like a purse, or if it shows signs of wear, there is no need to keep it.

Purses make it possible to take items with us. They are the underpinnings of portability.

***

How portable is your faith? Does it go with you everywhere? Or do you reserve it for church or the designated time you read your Bible? Maybe when your life is rolling along and things seem pretty good, you feel like God is near—even if you've been neglecting him a little.

However, when a crisis hits, what is the first thing we do? We ask everybody to pray, and we cry out to God for help. That's good, and yesterday we talked about how God is our Father and our friend. But if we aren't intentional about cultivating that relationship, our faith can get left at home or in church, unless we suddenly need it. And then it can be difficult to grab hold of.

If we fail to carry our faith into all areas of our lives and everywhere we go, it begins to fade. It's like an old book with crinkly, fragile pages that are hard to read. We forget what they say. Our hearts forget how to listen when God speaks. I'm not suggesting the need to keep a Bible in our purse, but I am suggesting the importance of an ongoing conversation with God. If we take steps to become intentional about our personal relationship with him, we'll discover his presence in all of our circumstances, and we'll more readily turn to him for advice.

Consider the Israelites, wandering around in the wilderness searching for their promised land, as our example. God instructed them to make a place of worship where he could come and dwell with them. He also instructed them to take this place, the tabernacle, with them wherever they went. God wanted to be able to live in the middle of their camp, no matter where they traveled.

God still wants to do that. He wants to come live in the middle of your mess, and he wants you to carry him with you wherever you go.

Lord, help me remember to take you with me wherever I go. Remind me that you want to go along, to be present in every area of my life. I want to become closer to you every day.

- List some areas in your life that you struggle to allow God into.

- Are there any areas you try to control?

- What sort of purse would you design for carrying God with you? Draw a picture of it. (We know he lives inside our hearts and minds, but this activity might help you deepen your understanding of the constant nearness of the Lord.)

Wardrobe Action

The beauty of a woman is not in the clothes she wears, the figure that she carries, or the way she combs her hair.

—Audrey Hepburn

- How many purses do you own?

- Do they all fit in your storage spot, or do you (or your husband) trip over them when you open the closet?

- Do your purses reflect your personal style rather than the current fad?

- Check each one for wear, and determine if it fits your current style. Eliminate those that no longer meet your standards. Consider whether it is in good shape and can be given away or sold, or if it just needs to be laid to rest.

DAY 10

Purse-stravaganza

Cast your burden on the LORD,
And He shall sustain you.
PSALM 55:22

We talked yesterday about purses as a personal style state-ment. Today I want to focus on the functionality of our purs-es. Trends fluctuate, but function remains a high priority. As I stated, my grandmother carried very different purses for separate functions. Do you do that too? Some women pre-fer to carry the same purse almost all the time because they don't want to keep changing out all the contents—and they have a lot of contents!

How big is the purse you gravitate to most of the time? Do you like a huge bag in which you can carry every item you might possibly ever need? Or do you prefer a smaller bag with only the essentials tucked inside?

I am a reformed huge-purse gal. There was a time when the thought of needing an item I failed to carry in my purse terrified me. Especially when my kids were little and I ditched the diaper bag for a diaper in my purse.

Then I got cancer. The chemotherapy left me too weak

to carry a purse at all. So I opted to hold my slim wallet, phone, and keys in my hand. That was it. Nothing else. It was either that, or my husband would have to carry a purse. He would have—he's that kind of husband. But I decided I could survive without all the extra trappings. I discovered after my treatment that I no longer desired to carry a big purse with a lot of stuff inside. I shopped for the smallest cross-body bag, in the most lightweight material, I could find. This turned out to be a quilted-fabric Vera Bradley purse.

I also discovered freedom with my decision. It was like a weight had been lifted off my shoulders, because it had. The occasional back issues I'd previously dealt with vanished. My heavy purse had been weighing me down for years, and I didn't realize it until I was forced to give it up.

Give some serious thought to why you carry the type of purses you do. Consider your wallet as well. Is it big and bulky, or slim? Is it compact, or is it a relic with space for a checkbook? Can you slip your wallet into any purse, or does the purse need to be a giant bag to accommodate your wallet? Do your purses weigh you down? Do you struggle with tired or sore back muscles, or worse?

**

Are you carrying a load in your mind or heart today? Do you lug around a burden that is difficult to handle on your own? You can decide to give it up and let stronger shoulders carry it for you. That's the kind of father and friend God is. He's walking right beside you and wants to take your burden, your worry. All you have to do is tell him about it and then hand it over.

The problem with the above advice is that it often

terrifies us to give up control. Like the security of a huge purse, we want to make sure we're ready for any possibility. We can be afraid to trust God with our issues, almost like we're afraid he might not have a big enough bag to carry all our *stuff*.

However, we really can trust him. He wants to carry our burdens, like my husband would have if I'd let him. This analogy only goes so far, because while it was fine for me to simply carry fewer items and refuse his help, that strategy doesn't work out so well with our emotions and cares. We can't just decide to leave them behind. We need to hand them over to the only one who can really help us.

Lord, I confess I carry around all my burdens. I don't want to do that anymore. I want you to take the things I've been worrying over and trying to control. They're too heavy for me.

Heart Action

- Write down what is bothering you today, what worries you.
- Write a prayer beside each one, giving control of it over to God.
- Draw a picture expressing the freedom and lightness you feel.

Wardrobe Action

Fashion is not necessarily about labels. It's not about brands.
It's about something else that comes from within you.
—Ralph Lauren

- Evaluate the purses remaining in your closet for function. Are any so large they might cause back strain?
- Pull out your wallet. Does it meet your current needs, or does it contain compartments for items you no longer use or carry? Does it have enough slots for all your cards? Can you easily fit a dollar bill lengthwise into it? Does it accommodate change?
- Do you need to make any changes? If so, document them.

Scarf It Down

Now all who believed were together,
and had all things in common.
ACTS 2:44

A scarf can be the final added touch to an outfit that sets it off. Just like other areas of fashion, popular styles of scarves change with the times. Preferred fabrics range from yarn to silk to cotton; patterns might be bold and bright or mini prints, stripes, dots, flowers, or plaid. The fad one season will be long and flowing, and the next be small and tied close to the neck.

The nice thing about scarves is that you don't need to pay a lot of money to get one that looks fabulous. That's not to say there aren't some worth paying a big price for; but generally, scarves are one of the least expensive accessories that give a lot of bang for the buck. So it is easy to keep up with the times in scarf style.

Keep a couple of things in mind when choosing a scarf. The first is the color. This will be the accent color closest to your face, so it needs to be a flattering hue for you. Another consideration is bulk. If you are aiming for a slim silhouette, a bulky wool or knitted scarf may not be best. Remember, extra fabric can look like extra you.

I mentioned some scarves are worth an extra investment. These would be more like wraps. They might be cashmere or silk and will add warmth around your upper arms. They could also be an elegant addition to a sleeveless evening dress.

I own one scarf in each of these categories. My cashmere wrap is wonderful for summer when the indoor temperature is cool and for travel when airplanes feel cold. It fits into my carry-on bag without taking up as much space as a jacket. I also own a long, black, sheer scarf with opulent beading at the ends. I wear it as a wrap for more formal occasions.

If you wonder how to tie a scarf, search for YouTube video tutorials to help.

With just a little attention to style and a little money invested, scarves can make your outfit come together with added polish and zest.

Scarves are also more dispensable than other, more costly wardrobe pieces. You don't need to keep a scarf you don't love anymore or that is obviously out of date.

If care isn't taken to store them properly, scarves can overrun your closet. They either fall off shelves, or swing in your face if you've hung them on the door. Or they slip off the hanger into a pile on the floor. They can be unruly. Organization is key to enjoying your collection.

***

Can you identify some unruly, difficult-to-manage areas of your life? Do you wear your worry like a cozy wrap around your shoulders, and then struggle to put it away? Is flamboyant energy exhibited in public a distraction from the pain in your soul? Do you find it difficult to take off the facade? Do you prefer spending time in your closet corralling pieces of your life to going out and living it? Do words just seem to fly out of your mouth without passing between your ears?

Our thoughts and emotions, like scarves, can become a slippery, tangled-up, and out-of-control mess. Or they can be a beautiful addition to the feminine life. It all depends on our management strategies.

Scarves are best stored rolled up and standing close together. Community in the scarf drawer or box is ideal. It is also ideal for us to live in community with others. Those closest to us help us stay on track. They can keep us from falling off the shelf or slipping off the hanger. And they come alongside to help us sort out the mess when the worst happens.

The Bible talks about this concept a lot in the book of Acts. The people of the early church spent almost all their time together. They even sold personal property and pooled their money to help each other. Today we might live independent lives, but we need at least one person who can hold us accountable for our spiritual disciplines. We also need to worship with others on a weekly basis, and we need to absorb what God says in the Bible every day.

Acts is not the only place where the Bible describes living in community. The Israelites also lived all together in one place in the Old Testament. They were instructed to live apart from peoples who did not worship the one true God so their faith would not become diluted. We don't live in communes, usually, and I'm not suggesting it. But close community with other believers is still important. It's the drawer space where we can roll up.

Lord Jesus, I realize if I try to live life on my own, without other people, I'll be like a pile of scarves on the floor—a tangled mess. Remind me of the importance of community. Help me find at least one person to whom I can be accountable. Thank you for designing the church as a community of believers. I want to become a more vital part of my local community of faith, both in giving and receiving.

Heart Action

- Find at least one person to whom you can become accountable. (This person will ideally not be your spouse. And as women, you really need another woman in this place.)

- Find at least one person (perhaps the above person) for whom you can provide accountability.

- Set a lunch or coffee date with this person.

- Is there a dangling, unruly area of your life that you need to roll up? Something that feels out of control? Spend some time asking the Lord to help you. Bring this problem up with your accountability partner. Together, search Scripture for verses that might offer help. A few of my favorites are Romans 12:1–2; Proverbs 23:7; and Philippians 4:8.

Wardrobe Action

You're never fully dressed without a smile.
—Little Orphan Annie

- If your scarves have taken over your closet, find a drawer or box for them. Roll each scarf and stand the rolls in rows.

- Go through your scarf collection. Lay aside those you don't wear or don't like. Pull out any with snags, stains, or other imperfections.

- Throw away the snagged and stained scarves. Give away the other rejects.

Part 2

REFRESH YOUR STYLE

Do Your Research

These words are faithful and true.
REVELATION 22:6

All Scripture is given by inspiration of God,
and is profitable for doctrine, for reproof,
for correction, for instruction in righteousness.
2 TIMOTHY 3:16

Nobody wants to look like they dress in outmoded styles or their mother's jeans. If you do not add any new pieces to your wardrobe for years in a row or pay attention to current styles, eventually it will happen—you'll become the one dressing in styles from a decade ago. The nice thing is, you don't have to spend a lot of money or go out and buy a whole new wardrobe each season. The key is education. You need to know what is current in order to evaluate what you already own.

Research is one of my favorite parts of maintaining fashion expertise. I love paging through magazines and perusing Pinterest, Instagram, and other websites. Each fall and spring I read reports of the runway shows and take notes from rundowns of the trends. It is a rare occasion when I see something on the runway that I would actually wear. But certain elements will stand out that I can incorporate into my personal style.

I also check out popular paint colors each season. You might be surprised at this. However, color crosses into all design areas—fashion, beauty, advertising, and interior design. The Pantone Institute of Color is the master of this concept. Their *Color of the Year* will show up in all four areas, and they even offer products to help designers integrate a particular season's colors into their businesses.

If this all seems a bit much for you, never fear. I distill my research into manageable bites in blog posts on my website at kathryngraves.com.

The next step after research is deciding what you like and what you don't like. Ask yourself which current trends express your personality. Those are the ones you'll adopt. No rule says that just because something is trendy, you must wear it. Also, there are no rules about how to wear trends. For example, if you notice that English garden flowers are popular, enjoy the freedom of attaching a flower pin to your shoe, if you choose. Put your personal stamp on style.

※ ※ ※

Just as dressing in style requires research, so does living the Christian life. And just like it can be either fun or tedious, depending on your outlook, to research fashion, Bible study can also seem either fun or tedious. The key is knowing yourself. Do you enjoy digging deep to pull out hidden meanings, or do you prefer the bigger picture? While both are important, the good news is that other people have done a lot of the work for you if you just don't have time or the inclination to dig deep. There are many good commentaries and other books that will help you when you come across something you don't understand.

But nobody is exempt from needing to read the Bible every day. It doesn't matter if you decide to read the whole thing in one year, or if you want to take it in smaller chunks. What matters is that you read it. Daily. This is how you learn how God wants you to think and how to live out your faith. Style is not just about clothes. It is about how you act and carry yourself. It touches your whole life. You know—lifestyle.

The New Testament is particularly relevant on this point, because it was written in large part to teach the first Christians how to live like Christians. The Old Testament is also important because it teaches us what God is like, how he interacts with people, and what his promises are.

Do you have a favorite Bible verse? Maybe you even have a life verse—one that you've chosen as the theme for your life. Many people choose a word or a verse for each new year. A good challenge is to memorize verses, or even whole chapters, from the Bible. This is difficult for me, so I print them out on sticky notes and note cards. I put them up around my house and in my car where I can see them. Maybe I can at least learn them by osmosis!

Romans 10:8 says, "'The word is near you, in your mouth and in your heart' (that is the word of faith which we preach)." Then verse 17 says, "So then faith comes by hearing, and hearing by the word of God." The point is that God's Word is paramount for a life of faith. First Timothy 4:6 goes so far as to say we are "nourished in the words of faith."

Genuine personal style is something that radiates from your soul. What you wear is a reflection of what is inside your heart. And it is this inner self that craves the Word of God like a juicy steak.

Lord Jesus, I want to learn how to live a life that pleases you. Help me as I make the commitment to read the Bible every day. Speak to my heart and teach me from your Word.

Heart Action

- Look for a Bible reading plan that suits you. Maybe you want an in-depth study of a book in the Bible. Maybe a monthly chart of a verse a day is more your style. Or maybe you'd like to read the Bible through in a year. Drop by your local bookstore or search the internet. You'll find many Bible reading plans. Make some notes about possible plans.

- Ask a friend or relative to read along with you. As we learned yesterday, there is great value in accountability. This year, my whole church is reading through the Bible together using the same plan. Talk about accountability!

- As you read, ask yourself, *What does this passage say? What does it mean? What is God saying to me?* Journal the answers.

Wardrobe Action

Don't be into trends. Don't make fashion own you,
but you decide what you are, what you want to express
by the way you dress and the way you live.
—Gianni Versace

- Begin your research into this season's style trends. Browse magazines and websites that interest you. If the idea of research overwhelms you, search for blogs like mine that will break it down for you.

- Make a list of your favorite magazines and sites here.

Color Code

All the women who were gifted artisans spun yarn
with their hands, and brought what they had spun,
of blue, purple, and scarlet, and fine linen.
EXODUS 35:25

Today we'll get down to the nuts and bolts of what to look for in our research on fashion. In this chapter we'll discuss color and pattern.

Each year Pantone decides on a single color that will dominate all areas of fashionable design. More often than not, the industry agrees and it shows up everywhere. Also, paint makers put out what they believe will be their most popular hues each year. The statistics they use to come up with these choices are usually on point, partly because consumers buy what they are led to believe is *in*. When we put all this together, we come up with a relatively solid idea of what will be a popular color palette in any given year. Within this over-arching spectrum lie individual seasonal favorites.

After getting a concept of the color spectrum, research becomes more fun. Pinterest and Instagram are filled with pins and posts from street stylists who riff on the colors in fresh, maybe even unexpected ways. I never recommend copying anyone's style exactly, but picking and choosing from these sites can liven up anybody's style sense.

Once you know what colors to use, express your style by creating your own color combinations. Some experts suggest limiting your color palette to a select few. I could never do that to my wardrobe. I love a variety of colors and want them all—all of the time.

Pattern is an area of color combining. Graphics and florals alike utilize color. Pay attention to whether the current season is filled more with one or the other. As I write this, stylized flowers in bold colors, along with anything plaid or striped, are hot. So are logo tees and sweatshirts. A few seasons ago, dots were all the rage.

Becoming familiar with the colors and patterns helps us remain current. I remember a time when pastel blue and mauve pink were the hot combination. In those days, we couldn't imagine putting blue with brown. But that's exactly what was popular in the previous decade, and this combo has come around again. In the 1980s, and again today, English country garden florals were the flower graphic of choice. This is at least partly a reflection of British Royals mania. So you see how it is not only fashion icons who decide what's popular, but societal trends as well. It just never pays to put your head in the sand and ignore the world around you, either in fashion or in life.

***

Where does color come from? What is its source? God created the world for us to live in, and he created us in his own image. Because of the variety of color in the natural world, we can assume that color pleases the Lord—maybe even that he enjoys looking at it and being surrounded by it.

The Bible describes God's plan for color to be utilized in the tabernacle and the temple. Rich reds, blues, and purples adorned both, along with gold and silver. Revelation 4:2–3 describes the rainbow quality of colors around God's throne in heaven. Turn to that passage and read about it.

A rainbow is a pattern of stripes. The bare branches of trees in winter crisscross each other in living plaid. And flowers are displays of vibrant colors. Jesus has been described as the Lily of the Valley and the Rose of Sharon.

No matter the season or climate type where you live, color abounds. Winter zones might be more subdued in their natural color scheme, but color isn't missing altogether. Jesus taught his disciples to pay attention to flowers and their beauty: "Consider the lilies of the field, how they grow: they neither toil nor spin; and yet I say to you that even Solomon in all his glory was not arrayed like one of these" (Matthew 6:28–29). While Jesus was making a larger point here, he did acknowledge the beauty of floral color.

What do colors in the world around you say to you about God? Do they lead you to praise him? Do they lend you a grateful heart? Perhaps colors help you see, in your mind's eye, the glory of the Lord.

Royal reds, blues, and purples remind me of the supremacy of God. And all the variety of color in the world makes me thankful for the one who is interested in the smallest details—even the details of my life.

Lord, I praise you for your creative greatness. Thank you for providing a world of color for us to live in. Each time I think about a color, help me remember how much you love me.

Heart Action

- With colored pencils or markers, draw a series of color patches. Make them the colors of the rainbow or the royal colors used in the tabernacle. Next to each color patch, using that color pencil or pen, write a word that describes God. Let the colors help you choose the words. For example, I would scribble a red patch and then write *Savior* beside it.

- Draw a picture or graphic design with your chosen colors to illustrate something you love about God. (Alternative: draw a scene from nature that inspires you.)

- Pray a simple prayer praising God for the attributes you listed.

Wardrobe Action

Elegance is not standing out, but being remembered.
—Giorgio Armani

- Using your colored pens or pencils, make a color palette with your favorite colors.

- Look through your clothes to see if all, or at least some, of your favorite colors are represented. Since your wardrobe should reflect your personality, the colors in it need to be ones you like.

- Write down or draw a color swatch of the current Color of the Year.

DAY 14

The Long and Short of It

O LORD, You have searched me and known me.
You know my sitting down and my rising up;
You understand my thought afar off.
… I will praise You, for I am fearfully and wonderfully made;
Marvelous are Your works,
And that my soul knows very well.

PSALM 139:1–2, 14

As seasons come and go, the popularity of certain wardrobe items waxes and wanes. Some years, button-down cotton blouses reign. In others, it's all about the knit tunic tee. Trends in pant lengths and widths also fluctuate, often from one extreme to another. Designers will throw all convention aside and take an unexpected tack, showcasing denim for dressy evening occasions, or formal pants suits. Another popular twist is skorts instead of shorts. Part of the job of a designer is to make enough changes from season to season that the consumer must buy new items. So even if we hold onto our favorites—because, after all, what goes around usually comes back around—the new version will come with a fresh approach.

So what is a cost-conscious woman to do? I'll address finances and budgeting in a later chapter. But for now, let's focus on how to know the difference between trends, fads, and personal style.

Any assessment must begin with research. Using the skills you've gained, check out the current trends. What type of top is featured most? Is it long or short? Tunic or blouse? Bulky sweater or more slim-lined? Blouson effect or baggy? Long, loose jackets and sweaters or fitted? Next, move to pants and shorts. Are they slim or baggy or boot-cut, high-waisted or low? Are shorts shorter or longer? Are capris or ankle pants more prevalent?

Armed with this knowledge, then consider what looks best on your particular figure. One important thing to remember: just because something is popular doesn't mean you have to wear it. However, you do want to wear some things that are popular. Take care as you choose from what's out there. Make sure the clothes you wear flatter your shape.

I am short and curvy. This is why I avoid long, straight, or baggy tops. I need to keep the hemline just below my hip or above it, and never let a top end at the widest part of my hips. I require some shape built into the top. If it is straight, my whole torso will look as large as my bust line. My small waist is completely hidden. However, I can incorporate some tunic tops over leggings. Some of them are built with seams following my natural curves. I also make a point to wear ankle-length leggings rather than capri-length. My calves are very large compared to the rest of my leg.

Maybe you are built more like a willow. Make your style selections ones that fool the viewer's eye into thinking they see curves. Choose hemline lengths to end in places you want to emphasize. If you're an apple shape, long, straight lines will disguise the larger size of your middle. You can plan your wardrobe to not only flatter your figure, but also incorporate style trends you see in your research.

We also need to take modesty into consideration. Just because runway models wear completely sheer clothes, doesn't mean we should. Think of it this way: the designers showcase extremes so we will get the message. Then it is up to us to add bits of their ideas to our clothing selections. Sheer sleeves carry the trend in a modest way. This example is true for all trends. Avoid the extremes and keep your personal image forefront in your mind.

＊＊＊

Do you wish you looked different than you do? I'm a chronic people watcher. I check out women in airports and stores to see what they're wearing. If a woman seems extra put-together, I try to figure out why. Is she naturally prettier, or does she simply know how to wear her clothes and accessories? Behind my people watching is the basic insecurity I feel about myself. I think most of us are insecure about at least one aspect of the way we look. When we study fashion trends, we only see thin models and assume that's what we need to be.

If you feel *less than* in areas of your life, be comforted by knowing God loves you as you are. After all, he created you. Psalm 139 is a beautiful passage confirming this truth. Please turn there in your Bible and read verses 13–17 now. While you are worrying about how you look, God is thinking good thoughts about you. He's thinking about how much he loves you, how he has made good plans for you. He thinks about how he wants to protect you and guide you.

He delights in walking alongside you throughout your days and watching over you at night.

There is no one else like you. You've heard it before, I'm sure—you're a masterpiece of God's creation. Let this truth sink in. Just sit and contemplate it for a few minutes. Then spend some time thanking the Lord.

Father, thank you for making me just the way I am. Thank you for loving me and watching out for me. Help me remember that you never make anything that isn't beautiful—including me.

Heart Action

- Write Psalm 139:13–17 in the space below.
- Decorate the margins and some of the words with colorful, pretty doodles.
- Write these verses on a notecard that you can stick to your bathroom or dresser mirror.
- Consider memorizing these verses.

Wardrobe Action

Fashion changes, but style endures.
—Coco Chanel

- Make a list of some current trends you discovered for tops and jackets/sweaters.
- Do the same for bottoms/skirts.
- Look through your closet for items that might be especially trendy. How often do you think you wear these items? Do they flatter your figure?
- Make notes here about what you find.

Now That You Know

*The woman then left her waterpot, went her way into the city,
and said to the men, "Come, see a Man who told me all things
that I ever did. Could this be the Christ?"*

JOHN 4:28–29

Now that you've done your research and know what's in style for the current season, this information will help inform your wardrobe choices. You have also paid attention to your basic body shape and know what flatters your figure. And you know what to avoid. So it's time to begin putting it all together. The one missing element is the image you want to project.

Are you a fun, sassy girl, or a more quiet, shy type? Do you prefer simple elegance or over-the-top feminine pieces? Do you gravitate to graphics or soft florals? Is color your thing, or do you prefer neutrals? Do you think you need to wear a lot of black? (Think again about black. Royal hues absorb light in the same way as black. That means they will make you look slimmer also. You don't have to stick with black!) Do you love chunky fashion jewelry, or is small fine jewelry more your style?

Your wardrobe choices, while staying up with current fashion, should above all reflect your personality. If you discovered a couple of days ago that the colors you love are missing from your closet, then a big element of your personality is missing too. If you have mostly business suits but harbor a passion for feminine dresses, another piece of you is missing. If you wear mostly jeans and tees but love to dress up, you need a few more pieces that will express this—even if it just means adding a top with a bit of extra bling.

Over time, by choosing with intention, you can develop a wardrobe in which each piece conveys something about your personality. While you may need to wear clothes to work that aren't your personal style, such as a uniform, your leisure time and weekend clothes should reflect your personal flair. And if you have the freedom to dress at work in whatever manner you choose, be sure to let the real you shine without saying a word.

I hope yesterday helped you realize how beautiful you are. The Lord wants you to live with confidence and certainty that you are his child and valuable. He wants you to share the source of your confidence with others too. First Peter 3:15 tells us, "always be ready to give a defense [explanation] to everyone who asks you a reason for the hope that is in you." This means that when others notice the spark of your personality shining, they might ask you about it. It's the perfect opportunity to tell them that the source of your flair or elegance (or whatever they've noticed about your style) is Jesus Christ. Yes, you're learning tips to help you look more put-together, but the real truth behind it all is the beauty of Christ. You're beautiful because he made you and lives inside of you.

Nicodemus approached Jesus to ask about the source of Jesus' power (John 3). Jesus answered that it was the Holy Spirit who empowered him. If you are a believer, the Holy Spirit lives in you too. And he will give you the power to share this truth with others.

At first, being so honest can be scary. But people really want to know. The world out there is trying to figure out what you have already discovered. Value, beauty, and confidence are only found in the presence of the Lord and in a relationship with him. As he works to make your personality a more accurate reflection of him each day, and you work to make your wardrobe reflect your personality, the people around you will notice. And they will ask. So be ready.

The more often you tell others the source of your confidence, the greater your confidence will grow. It's a never-ending, beautiful cycle.

Thank you, Jesus, for your Holy Spirit who lives in me. Thank you for the work you're doing to make me more like you. Please give me the courage to tell the reason for the hope inside me. May my unspoken language be one that draws others to ask. And may the words I say come from you.

Heart Action

- In order to be able to tell the reason for the hope in us, we have to know how it got there. Write a short version on a separate piece of paper. Include a few sentences about what your life was like before you met Jesus, tell the events surrounding the moment you put your trust in him, and then describe some of the changes you've experienced as a result of your decision.

- Attach that paper to this page. Then you'll always know where it is.

Wardrobe Action

What you wear is how you present yourself to the world, especially today, when human contacts are so quick. Fashion is instant language.

—Miuccia Prada

- One last time, look through the clothes in your closet. Do they represent your personality? Are they pieces you love? Do they help you look your best?

- Ask a friend to look in your closet. Ask her the same questions. Sometimes another person can be more objective.

- Remove anything remaining that doesn't meet your expectations or project an image you intend.

Combo Punch

Create in me a clean heart, O God,
and renew a steadfast spirit within me.
PSALM 51:10

Sometimes we can get stuck in a rut when pairing colors in our wardrobe. For instance, we always put the floral cardigan with the same camisole or tank because the dark neutral of the under layer doesn't compete with the outer layer. But mixing it up can create a fresh vibe.

I own a white spring cardigan with a royal blue, yellow, and black floral design. For several seasons, I wore it with a black tank underneath. This was a safe, predictable combination that worked. But one day, as I was thinking how tired I'd become of some of my clothes, I decided to take a risk. I paired the sweater with a royal blue blouse cinched at the waist by a skinny red belt. The effect was stunning—and more flattering on my figure.

Each season, new color combinations turn up on the runways. If we look for those as we do our research, we can take the information to our closets and put it to work with what we already own. A recent trend as I write is blush pink with baby blue—a combo listed as the Color of the Year at Pantone for 2017. It was the first time two combined colors had topped that list. Noticing it was such a strong trend, I looked in my closet and discovered I owned a blush pink blouse that I usually wore with a black blazer and gray pants. So I decided to change it up. I opted for a matching pink blazer (that I purchased) and paired the blouse and blazer with faded bootcut blue jeans and brown booties. Then I added a soft blue leather cross-body purse. I accented the outfit with a black leather short necklace and blue stone pendant. Voila! My own take on the pink and blue trend.

One season I noticed mustard gold paired with baby blue. Another time, red and orange together showed up everywhere. Some years pastel combos reign, and some years brighter, bolder hues are all the rage. A new thing seems to be pastels for fall.

* * *

Does your relationship with the Lord seem stuck in a rut? Do you repeatedly go through the same motions? Do you read your Bible and pray each day and go to church on Sundays, all without feeling close to God? Does it seem like he doesn't hear your prayers, let alone answer them?

We all go through seasons like this. It's sort of like climbing a mountain. There are plateaus along the way where we can rest from the arduous uphill trek. Because they're comfortable, and higher than previous spots, we can fool ourselves into thinking we've gone as far as we can or even need to go.

The cure for a pause on a hike is to get up and con-tinue. The cure for a wardrobe rut is re-evaluation and a bit of change. The cure for a spiritual rut is to re-evaluate where we are and how we got there. Often, confession is needed to remove the muck from our boots. We need a fresh wind of hope and inspiration from the Lord. Confessing our apathy (or any sins we can think of) is a good place to start. The next step is to ask God to reveal any other sins to us, things we have become so accustomed to that we don't even recognize them as sin. As we read our Bibles, sometimes words suddenly jump out at us and we realize some routine patterns of thought or behavior are not what God desires from us.

Confession creates the upward momentum of our spiritual hike. It is a rejuvenating, fresh punch of color to a bland spiritual experience. On day six, you confessed the obvious things, but today consider taking it to the next level. Think about any ruts you might be in, any behaviors or attitudes that you might previously have ignored.

The wonderful thing is, when we confess our sins, Jesus will forgive us. It doesn't matter how bad we think they are or even how small or insignificant. Remember, "If we confess our sins, He is faithful and just to forgive us our sins and to cleanse us from all unrighteousness" (1 John 1:9). So don't be afraid to take the next steps. Ask him to show you the summit again and to refresh your tired spiritual life.

Father, I confess there are things in my life that need to go. I'm in a rut and have become blind to the truth in some areas. Help me lay them down, change my thoughts and behaviors, and move forward with you. Thank you for promising to forgive me.

- On a piece of paper, make a list of the things you know you need to confess.

- Ask the Lord to show you any other areas where sin may hide. Add those to your list.

- Pray, confessing each sin and asking Jesus to forgive it.

- Tear up your list and destroy it.

- Thank God for the fresh color combo of confession and forgiveness adding zing to your soul.

Wardrobe Action

I feel very strongly that clothes that fit well make a person feel better.

—Jil Sander

- What color combinations are fresh for the current season?

- Do you like these colors? Do they flatter your natural coloring?

- Choose one fresh combination and look for any items in these colors in your closet.

- Have you ever worn some of these items together?

- Can you pair at least two items that you've never worn together?

Combo Punch — Part Two

Without ceasing I make mention of you always in my prayers.
ROMANS 1:9

Yesterday we talked about how fresh color combinations can bring your current wardrobe up to date. Today we'll take the idea of fresh combos a bit further. Just like colors morph with the seasons, so do the cut and shape of clothes. Along with this change, we often can observe unusual pairings of shapes and fabrics.

With wide-leg pants, a trench coat might be the popular jacket of choice instead of a shorter option. Leggings that formerly were worn only with tunic-length tops might be worn with shorter tops or jackets. (I'm not suggesting we adopt this trend.) Booties with dresses instead of pumps is a trend that shocked conventional wisdom a few years ago.

Fabric combinations can also add a surprising twist to outfits. Velvet with denim, or a tough leather motorcycle jacket with a soft, flowing skirt are good examples. In fact, a simple way to upgrade your style quotient is to pair tough, maybe more masculine, pieces with ultra-feminine ones. This explains the booties-with-dresses phenomenon.

One note of caution: make sure the combinations you create flatter your figure. High-top shoes with a mid-calf dress will not look good on anyone except a tall, thin figure. Also, remember the image you want to project. Every choice we make needs to reflect who we are.

But we can certainly have fun with our clothes. I know a couple of teens who enjoy wearing colorful socks as a surprising element of their outfits. I have an artist friend who pairs unusual jackets with her skirts and pants. Another friend will not shop at chain department stores for accent pieces. She wants to stand out as the only woman with an item. She turns shopping into treasure hunting.

You can treasure hunt in your closet. First, check out the current trends. Then decide on two types of items you want to put together. Say you like the tough/flirty combinations. Search your wardrobe for one top or jacket that might fall into the tough category. Maybe it has metal zippers or studs. Maybe it is leather or suede. It could be denim with metal buttons or snaps, or military-inspired army green with epaulets and cargo pockets. Then look for a dress, skirt, or pair of pants that is ultra-feminine. A skirt or dress might be long and gathered or have lace or sheer trim. Pants might be velvet or floral patterned, or even chiffon.

Also remember that age really has nothing to do with expressing your personality. I love the style of one lady I know who is in her eighties and usually among the first to adopt fresh trends. She has a fun, spunky style and loves longer gathered skirts, belts, and jackets with plenty of bling or zippers and studs. She accents her style with colorful jewelry.

Yesterday we talked about one element of prayer that invigorates and freshens your spiritual life. Today, I want to address a combination. Intercession and petition are two elements of our praying that really do go together all the time, sort of like tops and bottoms. No matter what the tops and bottoms look like, if you wear one, you wear the other. The difference with intercession and petition is that sometimes we do utilize one without the other. While this doesn't produce prayer failure the way it would produce outfit failure, our lives will be richer and more productive if we pray both kinds of prayers.

Intercession is defined as praying for others. We do this almost by instinct. When a friend or loved one is ill or experiencing a tragedy, we ask God to help them. This is a good practice. But did you know you can also pray Bible verses for people? One of my favorites is, "Peace I leave with you, My peace I give to you; not as the world gives do I give to you. Let not your heart be troubled, neither let it be afraid" (John 14:27). When someone I'm praying for is upset or anxious about her situation, I pray this verse and insert her name instead of the word *you*.

If a person is engaged in a mind battle, I pray, "Casting down arguments and every high thing that exalts itself against the knowledge of God [in _____'s mind], bringing every thought [of _____] into captivity to the obedience of Christ" (2 Corinthians 10:5–6).

The possibilities are endless. So let me encourage you to not only pray what is on your heart for people, but to search out a Bible verse to pray for them.

Praying for ourselves and our own needs is considered

petition praying. We usually do this in a crisis. But we don't tend to pray for ourselves when everything is going well. Let me encourage you to find verses to pray for yourself. I particularly like, "I pray that the eyes of [my] heart may be enlightened, so that [I] will know what is the hope of His calling, what are the riches of the glory of His inheritance in the saints, and what is the surpassing greatness of His power toward us who believe" (Ephesians 1:18–19 NASB). These verses remind me of my standing in Christ.

When we appropriate the power of Scripture in our praying, and when we apply it to both intercession and petition, we are refreshed. We gain confidence. We become able to rest in our trust in the Lord. And we are introduced to a new combination that works every time.

Dear Lord, thank you for your Word. Thank you that I can come before you with my needs and the needs of those I care about. Help me remember to use the power of Scripture as I pray. Thank you in advance.

- Look up a Bible verse you can pray for each member of your immediate family.

- Look up a verse to pray for yourself.

- Write these verses next to each person's name below.

- Each day, as you pray for others and yourself, begin with these verses.

Wardrobe Action

Fashion has always been a repetition of ideas,
but what makes it new is the way you put it together.
—Carolina Herrera

- Decide which two styles you want to combine.

- Pull pieces out of your closet that fall into these two categories.

- Try different combinations until you have found at least one that you've never worn before.

The New You

*I beseech you therefore, brethren, by the mercies of God,
that you present your bodies a living sacrifice, holy, acceptable
to God, which is your reasonable service. And do not be
conformed to this world, but be transformed by the renewing
of your mind, that you may prove what is that good and
acceptable and perfect will of God.*

ROMANS 12:1–2

Now that you've begun creating new outfits from the items already in your closet, a whole new world will open up to you. I'm sure you realize you can't just grab something out and put it on without first working to achieve your desired effect. The process requires practice and thought. But hopefully your personality is beginning to shine through.

The object is to develop a personal style that transcends seasonal trends. While you want to include items to reflect current fads, you can do so with smaller, less expensive items such as accessories. Longer-term trends can be reflected in more substantial pieces. And like my eighty-something-year-old friend, you can discover your own flair.

I gravitate to more classic, understated styles in clothes,

but then add bling and zing with standout accessories. I've even been known to buy clothes to go with my jewelry!

One obstacle I had to overcome was my age. I somehow thought that after I turned forty, I couldn't dress with current fashion anymore. Thankfully, that myth has been blown to bits. We now see women of all ages as fashion models and in TV commercials.

Another myth is that of size. A gal of any size can develop her own style and be in style. The good news is that designers, manufacturers, and advertisers have all begun to realize their prejudice against heavier women and are producing stylish clothes in larger sizes.

Even shoe companies are getting in on the act. I have a wide foot and large calves. For years, all I could find in shoes that fit properly were what I called *old-lady shoes*. In recent seasons I've even begun finding what I call orthotic shoes in designer styles. This year I found a pair of tall brown boots that are comfortable without any modifications. Up till now, I could not find a pair I liked that would fit around my calves without being a whole size too large for my feet.

I hope you enjoy playing with your clothes to discover fresh outfits from pieces you already own. You can arrange pieces in the new outfits on your bed, or you can buy a mannequin to assist your explorations.

You can invite a friend over to help you play too. Then go to her house and play in her closet. If you can view the process of building a wardrobe that expresses your personality as play or dress-up games, you'll enjoy it instead of dreading it.

× × ×

As we've breathed new life into our closets, we've also

discovered ways to jump-start or rejuvenate our spiritual journey. While discipline is important to keep us on track, would you describe your relationship with God as fun?

I think too often we focus so much on what we think we're supposed to do that we forget it's not supposed to be boring or drudgery. There is freedom in Christ, not bondage to rules: "Stand fast therefore in the liberty by which Christ has made us free, and do not be entangled again with a yoke of bondage" (Galatians 5:1). God is not boring. He doesn't think we are, and we don't need to think he is either. He is the most interesting being ever. And his goal is to set us free.

Free from what? Freedom from legalistic rules, from false thoughts satan has planted in your mind from expectations others place on you, and from pressures you place on yourself. He died to set you free from the penalty of sin and its hold on you—we call these strongholds. Anything that keeps you discouraged, depressed, or feeling helpless needs to be placed in God's hands and given up to his control.

If your mind's default setting becomes praise and thanksgiving, and you take all your anxieties and cares to the Lord for him to handle, your life will explode with joy and freedom. This is the real you.

Your real style is invigorating, peaceful, joyful, and thankful. Let these be reflected through your wardrobe style choices and on your face. Let the world see the brand-new you.

Jesus, thank you for setting me free from bondage of any kind. Thank you for making me new. Help me remember my freedom any time I am bombarded by depressing or defeating thoughts. These are not from you, and I don't have to let them stay in my mind. Help me keep my focus by reading the Bible and defaulting to thoughts of praise.

Heart Action

- Look up several Bible verses that praise God. The book of Psalms is a great place to start.

- Any time you begin to think negative or defeated thoughts, read these verses out loud.

- If there is a stronghold of sin in your life or thought life, ask God to remove it and find a verse you can pray to claim freedom over it.

- Rejoice in the new you God has created. "Therefore, if anyone is in Christ, he is a new creation; old things have passed away; behold, all things have become new" (2 Corinthians 5:17).

Wardrobe Action

Style is very personal. It has nothing to do with fashion. Fashion is over quickly. Style is forever.
—Ralph Lauren

- Set aside some time today to play in your closet. Work out at least one new outfit. Make notes about it below.

- Try to define your personal style in a few words—or even just one word.

- This will become your outline. When you shop for new pieces, remember to look for items that reflect your style.

A Whole Other Closet?

Put on the whole armor of God,
that you may be able to stand against the wiles of the devil.
EPHESIANS 6:11

Do you have in your house a whole closet devoted to coats and outerwear? I grew up in the Midwest, and we had a closet where we only hung our coats. It was located near the front door so we could grab a coat on the way out or easily put it away upon returning home. Every member of the family kept their coats in this closet instead of the closet in their bedroom. After I married, we lived in the South. The coat closet idea seemed foreign to most of my friends in that region. It simply wasn't needed in the warmer climate.

This brings us to the item of clothing we haven't discussed yet—coats. Fashion trends in outerwear change as often as they do for other clothes. But a coat requires a significant investment. It's not something most women change out every year. How can we stay up with current fashion and still wear the same coat several years in a row?

Outerwear is one area where we want to avoid fads and focus on long-term style. By keeping to the principles we've already learned about how to choose pieces that look best on our figures and colors that flatter us, we can be confident in our outerwear choices. However, we also need to consider the activities we'll engage in while wearing a particular coat.

With this in mind, consider where you need to wear coats. Will you primarily wear it to work? Will it be your ski/snow sports coat? Or will it be what you toss on over jeans and a sweatshirt on the weekend?

My suggestion is that if you live in a climate where a coat is needed, invest in two for winter and one for fall/spring. One winter coat will be a dress coat. This will be worn over dresses and dressier pants and to places a bit more upscale than a trip to the grocery store. The other winter coat will be for casual wear and could double as a ski coat. Some ski coats have a zip-out jacket inside them that can be worn on its own for not-quite-as-cold days. The fall/spring coat should be a trench coat, possibly with a hood for rainy weather.

Various other jackets can be worn, such as denim jackets, blazers, jogging wear, and motorcycle jackets, but those are pretty self-explanatory. You know which of those you prefer and which looks best on you. Just remember your personal style and your best colors and you'll be set.

For your dress coat, remember that while it needs to be as long as most of your dresses, it should not be too long. It certainly should not end at the widest part of your calves. The shape should flatter your figure. A swing coat can look fabulous on a tall, thin woman, but look like an old-fashioned maternity coat on a shorter, curvy woman. An apple-shaped woman will not want seams that curve in at the waist and out at the hips because the coat will not fit and will bulge and look bulky.

Your casual winter coat will be short—usually hip length. You want it to be long enough to keep out drafts, but short enough for ease of motion. The color should be more neutral. Avoid any color or pattern that will not endure. Black, tan, white, gray, navy blue, true red, and even some pastels will stand the test of time. The 2018 Color of the Year, Ultra Violet, probably will not.

The trench coat doesn't change much from one season to the next. Sometimes popular colors change, and sometimes they come in shorter or longer versions; but by definition, a trench coat has certain characteristics. It will button down the front, have a wide lapel, and be made of a fabric that resists water. Often, they are belted and have epaulets at the shoulders and a button tab at the sleeve opening. Sometimes a removable hood attaches under the collar. Think secret-agent look.

Colors for trench coats range from khaki tan or khaki green to the pastels, and sometimes black. A good one will last through many seasons.

***

Coats and other outerwear are our defense mechanisms against cold and wet weather elements. Do you have a spiritual defense? Let me explain what I mean by that. We're familiar with the term *defense mechanism* when we talk about our emotions. These are techniques we employ subconsciously to avoid emotional pain. One might go into denial, or lash out at the bearer of bad news, or try to make another person feel guilty for even thinking such things, etc.

These emotional defense mechanisms are not healthy and lead to further problems of their own making. What I'm talking about in the spiritual realm is a healthy defense against attack by the enemy, satan.

The Bible tells us our enemy is not another person or anything physical we can see. In 2 Corinthians 10:3–4 we read, "For though we walk in the flesh, we do not war according to the flesh. For the weapons of our warfare are not carnal but mighty in God." Satan will use the battlefield of our minds to wage intense warfare against us.

A favorite analogy of mine came from Adrian Rogers, a preacher. He explained that your mind is like an airport. Your will is the control tower. Thoughts are like airplanes. Satan will send a thought into your airspace that goes something like, *You're stupid. Anybody else would have seen that (whatever it was) coming.* Your will, acting as the control tower, can deny permission for that thought to land. Without permission, it will fly off to eventually run out of gas and crash. The only airplane thoughts your control tower needs to allow landing rights are those that line up with what the Bible says. God says you are fearfully and wonderfully made and precious to him (see Psalm 139).

I think we might believe we have no control over our thoughts. As I've shown you, we do. Our defense, according to Scripture, has parts like a suit of armor. Turn to Ephesians 6 and read verses 10–18 for the full description.

Lord Jesus, help me be strong as I combat the forces of evil that come against me like a rainstorm. Thank you for the weapons you gave us. I want to remember them and wear them every day.

Heart Action

- Make a list here of the armor pieces from Ephesians 6. Draw each one, if you like.

- Write out verses 14–17 on a notecard and place it as a bookmark in your Bible. Refer to it as needed in the heat of battle.

Wardrobe Action

There's never a new fashion but it's old.
—Geoffrey Chaucer

- Do you own coats you no longer wear? If so, consider giving them to a charity that helps the homeless, or an organization that helps battered women dress for job interviews as they begin new lives.

- Do you have a crammed coat closet or do you keep coats in your regular closet? Consider setting up a place exclusive to hanging outerwear if you live in a colder climate. An overhead shelf is nice for storing scarves and gloves, and for the coldest climates, space on the floor for snow boots is also helpful. I created space in my office closet for coats since our house doesn't have a coat closet.

- Pare your coat selection so that your space is not cram-packed.

- If you've held onto your coats for too many seasons and they look dated, consider making this the year you invest in new ones.

Part 3

PUT THE RIGHT THINGS IN

DAY 20

Hang-Ups

Cause me to hear Your lovingkindness in the morning,
For in You do I trust;
Cause me to know the way in which I should walk,
For I lift up my soul to You.

PSALM 143:8

If you want to avoid some trouble, you should put some thought into your hangers.

I admit it. The hangers in my closet are a twisted mess. I have never purchased wood hangers for my pants. For some unexplainable reason, I like the wire ones with cardboard tubes as the long bottom support. The tube seems shaped just right, and often has the bonus of a bit of stickiness on the cardboard to keep pants from slipping off. When the cardboard becomes bent, I toss the hanger and use a more recent gift from the dry cleaners.

The problem with these hangers is the wire part. I almost can convince myself that my hangers plot together at night to form a web so that when I open my closet in the morning, I can't pull out a pair of pants without doing battle against the hangers. And then my whole day gets off to a grouchy start.

I avoid placing pants on plastic hangers because they tend to sag in the middle over time. Then the pants form tiny gathers in the sides of each leg that remain upon wearing. I'm not a fan of ironing in the mornings, so these hangers just aren't an option for me—at least for pants. I love plastic hangers for tops and dresses.

Wood hangers are far and away the best option for pants. If you can find wood hangers with a ribbed rubber section where pants hang, so much the better. Another nice feature of wood hangers is their thickness. They force more space between items by their sheer size, helping to keep wrinkles at bay. There are all kinds of other configurations and materials for pants hangers, but none can compare to nice wooden ones.

As I previously said, plastic hangers are fine for tops and dresses. They are lightweight and often have little hooks for camisole straps, or indentions on the top for straps or to secure sleeveless items.

Skirts require their own style of hanger. I'm not referring to the plastic ones with which they might be sold. Those tend not to hang at the same level as other items, often hugging the closet bar. They sometimes are not big enough at the opening to even fit over a wood closet bar. And let's not even discuss wire hangers with clothespins.

My favorite style of skirt hanger is metal with two wood slats. A skirt waistband is placed between the slats, so it is sandwiched between them. There is felt on the insides of the slats to protect skirt fabric. A metal ring slides down the neck of the hanger to secure the slats in place. No pinched places form in the skirt fabric where clips press into it. Two skirts can be hung together without danger of one falling out. The main points to consider in skirt hanger selection are that skirts hang flat and that the hanger is easily maneuvered into and out of the closet.

* * *

Do you ever feel overwhelmed? As if no matter how hard you try to think right thoughts or read the Bible daily or pray, life just jumbles up? Almost like the pants hangers in my closet? Let me assure you, this is normal; but it doesn't have to become a pattern. Just like I know if I purchase the proper hangers, the pants section of my closet will stay in order, there are things we can do to minimize the overwhelming jumble of our lives.

Of course, you know I'm going to tell you the answer lies in the promises of God. Mornings set the tone of the day. A black-and-white charcoal painting on a wall in my bedroom reminds me of the right tone. It is placed beside my closet door. In the painting, a mama cat nuzzles the face of her kitten. The Bible tells us God is like the mama cat. He is that close. In Psalm 42:5 it says, "Why are you cast down, O my soul? And why are you disquieted within me? Hope in God, for I shall yet praise Him for the help of His countenance."

What is God's countenance, and how can it help us? A person's countenance is the expression on their face. The psalmist found comfort in the way God looked at him, in the presence of God's face next to his. Come close to him and allow his face to brush yours.

First thing in the morning, acknowledge God. Thank him for the new day. Ask him to come near. And then you can say with the psalmist, "Hope in God; for I shall yet praise Him, the help of my countenance and my God" (42:11). Your face will change because of the presence of God. Your mood will lift when you thank and praise him. If I didn't know better, I'd think the kitten in my painting is smiling. Just like that kitten, knowing God is alongside you as you go out to face the day will put a smile on your lips.

Lord, I give you my day today. Thank you for a brand-new day. Thank you for being close beside me, no matter what I might face. I will praise you for your help and goodness. I love you, Lord.

Heart Action

- Sit in quietness for a few minutes. In your mind paint a picture of a mama cat licking her baby's face (or use whatever animal you prefer).

- Read Psalm 42:5–11.

- Meditate on these verses and what they mean to you.

- Find a picture, or draw one, to fit the mama-and-baby image in your mind and place it below.

Wardrobe Action

Fashion is about dressing according to what's fashionable. Style is more about being yourself.
—Oscar de la Renta

- What sorts of hangers are in your closet? Do they function well? Are they attractive?

- Count how many pants hangers and skirt hangers you need to replace.

- Are your plastic hangers all different colors and styles? It can be nice to have all matching ones. Consider replacing ones that are bent or snag your clothes, at the very least.

- Schedule a shopping trip to buy new hangers according to the list you've made.

The Beauty of Drawers

*Let the words of my mouth
and the meditation of my heart
be acceptable in Your sight, O LORD,
my strength and my Redeemer.*

PSALM 19:14

We can think of drawers like we do file cabinets. They exist to corral important items in an orderly manner and make it easier to find those items. The problem with dresser drawers is that they don't usually come with dividers and tabs. Once we place clothes in a drawer, there is nothing to keep them from getting tossed around and scrambled.

We touched on the subject of drawers when we addressed foundations, but let's go a bit further today. What items belong in drawers, and what is the best way to fold and otherwise store those items?

Foundations, socks, hosiery, and sleepwear, along with sweaters, workout clothes, and shorts, are the things for which you'll want to make space. If you own a lingerie chest, bras, panties, socks, and hosiery each get their own drawer. If you're working with a dresser or chest of drawers, you'll need to combine more than one item in a drawer. In this case, I recommend bras, panties, and hosiery share a drawer, with the possible addition of athletic and knee socks. I also recommend drawer dividers to keep items separate from each other. As I'm sure you know, bra straps like to tangle with tights.

However, proper placement helps minimize tangles. Pretend you are in a department store. Lay your bras in your drawer the same way they appear on display tables in the store. They can overlap much like dominos from front to back in your drawer. Placing them at one end of the drawer minimizes their contact with other items and reduces the opportunity for tangles too.

The key to storing clothes in drawers, according to Marie Kondo, author of *The Life-Changing Magic of Tidying Up,* is to stand them on edge. You may be wondering how this can work with panties, socks, and hosiery. Her advice, which is almost miraculous in the space it saves, is to fold panties into rectangles. They will be small, of course, but then stand them in a row from front to back in the drawer next to the bras. The key to getting them to stand is to fold them small enough and to stack them from front to back.

Socks and other hosiery should be rolled up like sushi rolls. Longer items, like tights, can be folded in thirds first. Stand the rolls in a shoebox or use another divider placed in the drawer.

Give sleepwear its own drawer, but workout clothes can occupy the same drawer as shorts. The same principle applies, no matter what item of clothing you're working with. Fold it into rectangles, then in half and half again until you have a shape that will stand in the drawer. Line up the rectangles in each category from front to back in your drawer. Some fabrics or sleepwear might be too slippery, in which case you might want to roll the item like hosiery.

T-shirts, sweaters, blouses, camisoles, and tank tops can also be folded into rectangles and stored standing up in drawers if you have enough space. This will leave more room in your closet for pants, skirts, dresses, and jackets. But tops and cardigan sweaters can also be hung on hangers. Use your best judgment based on the drawer space you have and the room you gain by folding and storing items standing up.

I know what you're thinking. *This will take so much time!* Well, yes, it takes time. But the end result is so much less stressful, not to mention space-saving and wrinkle-reducing, that I think it's worth it.

***

Did you know your mind is like a file cabinet, or set of drawers with dividers? Everything we ever see, hear, or otherwise experience is stored up there. Some things are buried so far back that we may think we've forgotten them. But have you ever noticed how a certain smell or song can trigger a long-forgotten memory? It was still there, filed away or neatly folded and standing, waiting to be retrieved.

You might be wondering if every single bit of information that ever entered your mind really is still there. But I assure you, scientists know it is. And God knows too. Sometimes memories explode in living color at inopportune moments. Sometimes I can't coax a crucial bit of information to the front no matter how hard I try—until the middle of the night when I don't need it anymore. But God keeps track of it all. He knows every thought we think, every place we go, every movie or TV show we watch, every song we listen to, every website we visit, and every word we say.

It can be so easy to assume that no one knows certain things about us. That assumption makes us less cautious about our behavior and thoughts. So rather than chafe against the reality of God's omniscience, let's be grateful for it. Because he knows what goes on, it means he pays attention. And it means he cares.

Because we can never unsee something, or unhear it, or unsay words, let's be mindful of them ahead of time. Let's take the extra time and make the effort to consider them beforehand. Yes, it sounds like discipline, but the end result will be a cleaned-up mind and less *foot-in-mouth disease*. It will be life changing.

Father God, help me remember how important it is to guard my mind against damaging material, no matter what form it may take. Keep me ever aware of your watch and care over me. And when I haven't been able to control those things, grant me your grace to deal with them.

Heart Action

- If there are some damaging things in your mind, ask the Lord to cover them with his blood. Ask him to forgive you if you placed them there. If you are the victim of circumstances or words that someone else perpetrated on you, ask Jesus to help you forgive the person and to help you relegate the thoughts to the back files of your mind. If you need further help with the fallout, consider seeing a Christian counselor.

- There is no such thing as *forgive and forget*. So just because you remember, don't think it means you haven't forgiven. If you work through an issue once and honestly forgive, it is done and over—even if the other person won't let it rest. Their response is their problem.

- Sometimes it is only by the power of the Holy Spirit that we can push those damaging thoughts out of the front of our minds. One thing that does help is Bible memorization. It gives your mind something to do—sort of like work keeping a wayward child out of trouble.

- What is one Bible verse you can memorize to help you think the right thoughts? I like Philippians 4:8. Write it here.

Wardrobe Action

- Pull everything out of one drawer. Sort the contents into categories.

- Decide which categories to assign to each of your drawers.

- Fold into small rectangles (or rolls, as appropriate) the clothes that will belong in your empty drawer, and place them standing up in it.

- Repeat with each drawer.

- If you discover extra space, consider adding other categories to your drawers.

The Beauty of Drawers— Part 2

Trust in the Lord, and do good;
Dwell in the land, and feed on His faithfulness.
Delight yourself also in the Lord,
And He shall give you the desires of your heart.
Commit your way to the Lord,
Trust also in Him,
And He shall bring it to pass.

PSALM 37:3–5

Today, let's continue thinking about how to store things you don't want to hang in your closet. Drawers and dividers are perfect for clothing items. But what about accessories? What should you do with your jewelry, purses, belts, and scarves? Hopefully, your scarves are rolled up in their own cubby by now. Belts can be stored rolled up the same way. Purses and jewelry are another matter entirely.

Purses are a challenge to store. The ideal solution is to line them up on shelves, one deep, so you can see at a glance what you have. Stuffing with tissue paper helps retain shape, and the paper can hold the purse's place on the shelf.

I don't have as much available shelf space as I need for the purses I own, so I purchased a rack with hooks to hang over the door. Hanging them this way is not perfect, but at least it keeps them off of the floor. When I build a closet someday, I'll be sure to add shelf space for purses.

Jewelry can be a challenge to store. Fine jewelry should always be kept in a jewelry box or the box it came in. Necklaces need to be hung to prevent tangling the chains.

Fashion jewelry, while not as delicate as fine jewelry, still should be put in a covered place when not being worn. If it comes from the manufacturer in a plastic bag, this is a good storage option. Otherwise, stacking plastic trays can be used. Lay necklaces side-by-side with their chains fully extended. Never stack necklaces. Label the trays for necklaces, bracelets, earrings, and pins. If items come in a set, label a tray for those and keep the sets together. I go further and label gold, rose gold, silver, and beaded trays.

You can line the bottoms of your trays with velvet or other pretty fabric if you choose. Cut a piece of foam core board to fit, and wrap the fabric around it like a gift. Hot glue or staple the fabric on the backside of the board. If you use staples, be sure they don't protrude to the front of the board and snag the fabric.

The best option for these trays is a rolling cart they can slide into. This cart can be kept in a corner of any closet. Whatever option you choose for fashion jewelry, seeing what you have is paramount. Adequate labeling will help; but once you open the space, you need to be able to see what's inside. This is why I never recommend stacking items in a tray. What good is a piece of jewelry if you can't find it?

When we put our jewelry and other accessories away each night, we don't have to worry about what will happen to them while they're in storage. We know they're safe. If our thoughts and feelings are placed where they belong, in God's care, a sense of safety also comes. Psalm 37:3 tells us to trust in the Lord, dwell in the land, and feed on his faithfulness. We can take all our excess *stuff* to the Lord and leave it with him. He will keep it, and we will feel secure. Dwelling in a land and eating our fill sounds peaceful and enticing.

Just like when our clutter is up off of the floor and each item is in its place, filing away our worries in the care of the Lord produces calm in our minds. When we don't know what to do about something, the simple act of asking God about it takes the stress away. When we hand over our anxieties and worries, he manages them. He knows how our feelings need to be sorted out, and will take the time to help get the knots out.

Just like a jewelry box is no help at all if we don't put our jewelry in it, God can't help us if we don't take our issues and worries to him. He will only do what we allow him to do. But we can be sure he views our thoughts and feelings as precious gems and jewels. He wants to protect them.

Lord, I want to trust you. I need a safe place for my thoughts and emotions. I don't know what to do about many things I face. But you do. I know you love me, and I love you back. I commit right now to letting you handle my struggles. I know you'll show me the way forward.

Heart Action

- Draw a key that might unlock a beautiful antique jewelry box.

- In your mind, use the key to open a box for your thoughts and emotions.

- Imagine closing the box and handing the key to God.

- Spend a few minutes thanking God for his help and watchful care over the things that concern you.

Wardrobe Action

Real style is never right or wrong.
It's a matter of being yourself on purpose.
—Bruce Boyer

- Clean off a shelf and set your purses on it.

- Roll up and store belts in a shoebox or Christmas ornament storage box.

- Decide which method of jewelry storage you prefer, and make a list of items you need to purchase.

Lefty or Righty

Your ears shall hear a word behind you, saying,
"This is the way, walk in it,"
Whenever you turn to the right hand
Or whenever you turn to the left.

ISAIAH 30:21

Now that your closet is cleaned out and you only have the items you need hanging in it, there is still something to address—the way you hang those items. Let's break it down into pieces and begin with direction today.

Every item in your closet should face the same direction. If you're right-handed, face your clothes to the left. This way, when you reach up to grab a hanger, you'll pull it out with the front of the clothing facing you. If you're left-handed, face all your clothes to the right.

Why is it important to see the front of a top or dress first? Well, it just makes things easier. A big reason we've undertaken to clear out and clean up our closets is to make it easier to get dressed in the morning. If we can facilitate that ease by not having to flip or rotate our wrists to see what we've got hold of, so much the better. Have you ever noticed that stores hang all their clothes facing left? That's because most people are right-handed. Stores want us as customers to easily find what we want. Let's treat ourselves like the best customers at home.

Pants don't really have a left or right for hanging purposes. But skirts do. Hang them so the front of the skirt faces the same direction as your tops and dresses.

Some of us do this without even thinking about it. Others of us struggle with understanding the point and remembering to do it. My husband is one of the strugglers. When I open his closet, I can immediately tell which items he hung. They face the wrong way. He really does not understand my hang-up with direction in the closet. He doesn't care if he can see the front of a shirt first because he tosses it on the bed before he puts in on anyway. And once he takes it out of the closet, he'll wear it. End of story. No mind changing allowed. Take the time to face your clothes the same direction. You'll be able to look at and consider outfit choices without having to toss everything on the bed first.

* * *

The Bible has a lot to say about the direction of our lives. We're told to take direction from the Lord, to go in the right direction, and to go forward. But how do we know which direction is right for us? Is there a formula like there is for the closet?

Proverbs 3:5–6 tells us, "Trust in the LORD with all your heart, and lean not on your own understanding; in all your ways acknowledge Him, and He shall direct your paths." What are the keys to God directing us according to these verses?

The first is *trust*. We need to trust God with our hearts. We touched on that yesterday. We can trust God with everything we're concerned about in our hearts. If you gave him the mental key to your box, you've taken the first step.

The next is *lean*. Or really, *lean not*. Don't lean on your own gut instinct or rationale. This is where it can get tricky. Our feelings can fool us. And logic can be contrary to the way God wants to accomplish something. We absolutely cannot trust ourselves. We must do what it says next: *in all your ways acknowledge Him*. This is more than a quick wave and nod of the head. It is telling God we will do it his way. In order to do things his way, we need to spend time praying and reading our Bibles so we are open to his leading and can recognize it when we see or hear it. Because we will. *And He shall direct your paths*.

Lord Jesus, I want to hear your voice. I want to go in the direction you want for my life. Help me stay tuned in to you today. Show me the right way.

Heart Action

- Use a concordance (BibleGateway.com is one of my favorites) to look up several Bible verses about God's direction. Write the references in a notebook or journal.

- If there is an area of your life in which you need direction, no matter how small it may seem, write it in your notebook or journal.

- Add it to your mental jewelry box and hand God the key again.

Wardrobe Action

I am convinced that there can be luxury in simplicity.
—Jil Sander

- Turn all your clothes to face the same direction in your closet. This may require turning items around on their hangers. All hangers should also hang so the open side of the hook faces the rear of the closet.

Rainbows

Make me understand the way of Your precepts;
So shall I meditate on Your wonderful works.

PSALM 119:27

The second principle of organizing hanging clothes is color. Clothes should be hung grouped by color and moving from darker hues on the left to lighter on the right. If you have double-hanging rods, the clothes on the bottom rod should hang in the same color order as the clothes above. The exception is when the bottom rod is only for pants.

So, if you are a color person and own tops in a wide variety of colors, they need to be grouped so the blacks are together, then the browns, dark greens, dark blues, dark purples, reds, oranges, yellows, creams, pastels, and whites. When working with patterns, choose the predominant color to guide placement.

If you're more of a neutrals gal, your task might be easier since you don't have as many colors to organize. However, you may own many different shades of khaki and your creams might trend from pinkish to peachy. The variety may still be there, just in more subtle tones.

We want to organize by color—and hang in one direction—to ease choosing our clothes in the mornings. If we want to wear a certain color, we almost don't even have to open our eyes to find it. If you're like me in the morning, this can be a really good thing!

You may be wondering why the dark colors belong on the left, with light colors on the right. The answer has to do with psychology—for some reason, our brains like it better. The progression lends a sense of order and calm. Also, if your closet only has one regular door on hinges instead of sliding doors, it should open on the right. The first thing you want to see is light and bright, not dark and heavy. Your eye will also naturally travel from dark toward light. In a walk-in closet, as you face the rod on one side, if the lighter colors hang to the right, it lights the way for your eye to travel.

A bonus for hanging our clothes this way is a pretty closet. Let's face it, if our closets are ugly and out of sorts, we dread opening them to get dressed. But if they're clean, pretty, and colorful, the process becomes much more pleasant.

* * *

Our eyes are drawn toward the light for several reasons. Some are physical, having to do with the anatomy of the eye. Some are psychological and others spiritual. Jesus described himself as the Light of the world in John 8:12. In the same manner as our eyes are drawn to the sun our spirits are drawn toward Jesus Christ. And just like the sun illuminates the earth, Jesus illuminates our spiritual eyes so we can see truth and beauty, and he helps us see with our understanding what is not truth or beauty.

This discernment between truth and untruth is vital

to the Christian life. Unfortunately, many Christians forget to keep their closet door open and their minds and hearts in order. They are easily sidetracked by *stuff* they then toss aside into piles, or cram and jam the pieces of their lives together with no regard for peace and calm. We need to make space for Jesus, aligning our lives in such a way that our spiritual eyes travel easily toward our Light.

Just like in our closets, when we make a behavior pattern into a habit, it becomes easier to keep doing it. The first time we arrange our clothes by color, the pleasing effect helps us remember to keep doing it. Before we know it, we wouldn't dream of hanging yellows intermingled with purples. Our spiritual lives crave habits and patterns that lead us toward a more open, easy relationship with God.

Communication is the hinge. We listen by reading the Bible, meditating on verses, and memorizing them. We talk to God through prayer. As we do these things, our spiritual eyes travel the spectrum toward light. Our vision sharpens.

Do you know how to meditate on a passage? After you read it through, ask yourself what it means and what God is saying to you through it. Look for key words and focus on their meaning. Look for action words. What do they suggest or command? Pay attention to key concepts. You never know when a new light of understanding may dawn on you.

Lord Jesus, thank you for being the light of my life and world. I want to be a person who easily comes into your presence and whose mind is illuminated by your truth. Help me as I work to develop habits that will make this kind of life normal for me.

Heart Action

- Choose a Bible verse to meditate on today. Write it out in the space below.
- Doodle around key words or phrases.
- Read the verse out loud. Repeat, emphasizing one of the doodled words. Repeat, emphasizing a different doodled word. Repeat, until all doodled words have been emphasized.
- If you sense a message to you, write it after the verse.

Wardrobe Action

When in doubt, wear red.
—Bill Blass

- Arrange your clothes by color in your closet, moving from darks to lights, left to right.
- Close your closet door(s).
- Now open the door(s). Take a moment to note your psychological response to what you see.

Twins and Triplets

*So the ransomed of the L*ORD *shall return,*
And … they shall obtain joy and gladness;
Sorrow and sighing shall flee away.

ISAIAH 51:11

The last part of hanging clothes properly in the closet is to hang similar items together. This means categories of dresses, skirts, tops, jackets, cardigan sweaters (if you choose to hang them), and pants, with the possible addition of coats if yours will hang here. I have a double rod in part of my closet. Pants and skirts hang on the bottom rod with tops above them. Another section has a single rod at shoulder height. This is where dresses and longer tunic tops hang. My closet is very small, so I co-opted a nearby guest bedroom closet for jackets and sweaters and long-sleeve tops. I call this one my winter closet.

As you think about the categories for grouping, keep in mind the color grouping you did yesterday. You might need to rearrange items into several different rainbows. I have a pants color spectrum, a tops spectrum, a dress rainbow, and my winter closet is yet another color collection.

I still work to make sure the darker colors in a grouping are on the left, graduating to lighter ones on the right. But there is one more gradient to keep in mind—long to short. Within each category of clothes, as the color changes, try to also consider the length of the items. Place longer items on the left and shorter ones on the right. Does this mean you can't have a long white dress? No. But I think you'll find that your longer tops do tend to be the darker-colored ones. Many light-colored tops are camisoles and tanks that we wear underneath the bolder, darker colors.

No rule is absolute in the wardrobe, and this truth may be most evident here. You might really own a large number of light-colored, longer-length tunic tops or summer dresses. If you just can't organize for both color and item groups, choose one. The most important thing is not that you follow all the rules, but that you end up with a space that pleases you and makes it easy for you to choose outfits and get dressed.

Again, you may be wondering why shorter clothes go on the right. The same principle applies to length as to color. A gently sweeping arch of hemlines rising from left to right is pleasing to the eye and calming to the mind.

As we've worked together through this little spiritual journey, I hope you've noticed something. It is my prayer that you're developing habits that bring you into the presence of God with spontaneous joy. As we spend time with our heavenly Father, we allow him to fill more and more of our lives. The dark, ugly parts of us recede, and the light, beautiful rays of his love fill us up. Joy is the product of a well-ordered, God-tuned mind.

Joy is the one item we can pair with anything, and it will look and fit right. It is the layer, the wardrobe piece, we just can't go without. And it hangs nicely in our closets. It is that graceful, sweeping arch that lifts us and helps us look up. We read in Psalm 89:15, "Blessed are the people who know the joyful sound! They walk, O LORD, in the light of Your countenance."

Does your devotional life help you hear the joyful sound? Does it help you to see in the light of God's understanding?

Lord, thank you for lifting my mind and heart to a higher place filled with joy.

Heart Action

- Write the word *JOY* in the space below.
- Decorate it with designs and colors.
- Using a concordance, search for Bible verses containing the word. Make a list of them.
- Read one joy verse each day.

Wardrobe Action

Style is a way to say who you are without having to speak.
—Rachel Zoe

- Organize your closet so similar items are grouped together.
- Within each group, make sure the color progression remains dark to light and/or long to short, from left to right.

Re-evaluate: What Do You Have?

That their hearts may be encouraged, being knit together in love, and attaining to all riches of the full assurance of understanding, to the knowledge of the mystery of God, both of the Father and of Christ, in whom are hidden all the treasures of wisdom and knowledge.

COLOSSIANS 2:2–3

You have come a long way since we began. What a difference a few weeks can make! Today, as you open your closet, does it look full but not overflowing? Does it look calm and peaceful? Do you realize how much you still own?

Yes, I'm sure there are some gaps you still want to fill in, and we'll address that in the next couple of days. But I imagine you might be surprised at how much is still in your closet, even after all the major purging you did the first week. It fits better now, and looks a whole lot better. But you aren't left with nothing.

In fact, you have more. How is that possible? You now

have only pieces you will wear. You have what you know looks and feels good on your body. You don't have any extra stuff that only takes up space. And you can see what you have. Nothing will get stuck in the back or under other items and lost.

My husband's closet is a good illustration of this point. Due to poor design, it has one door on hinges. This door is less than two feet wide. His closet is four feet wide. This means the left half of his closet is a dark recess. Whatever clothes are hung there are out of view. I know what's there because I do the laundry and hang his clothes. But he forgets. He will only wear what is in the part he can see when he opens the door. If I never rearranged his clothes, he would never wear half of them.

This happens to us even if we can see our whole closet at once. Clothes become hidden, covered over, and stuck between other items, and we forget we even have them. So we never wear them.

That's why you now have more available to you than you did before you started cleaning out and paring down. So take a good look inside your closet today. Let it sink in just how much you still have to work with. Bask for a bit in the glow of a job well done.

***

You've done the same kind of work in your spiritual life as you have in your closet. You've cleared out what needed to go away and organized your private devotional time in a way that helps you see and focus on what's important. You've set some new priorities. And hopefully, you've gained a closer, more honest and open relationship with Jesus Christ.

Do you know what a treasure this relationship is? Do you realize how much you have? Just like with your clothes, you have more now than before—because you can see it. You've made space for what matters.

Think about your relationship with Jesus today. Consider things in the past that he's helped you get through. Meditate on your future with Jesus by your side. Do praise and thanksgiving well up in your heart? Are you at peace, with a sense of well-being?

Today is a day for gratitude for the things the Lord has done for us, through us, and in us. Even though there are still gaps we need to fill in, we already are so full of good and right things as a result of the mercy and grace of the Lord.

Thank you for all the wonderful things you've done for me, Lord. I praise you for how loving and merciful you are. I recognize the treasure I have in you. Thank you for the assurance you give me that I am rich in spiritual blessings.

Heart Action

- Make a list of some things you're thankful for.
- Turn this list into a prayer.
- Make a list of some of the attributes of God that have become meaningful to you in the last few weeks.
- Turn this list into a prayer.

Wardrobe Action

I want people to see the dress,
but focus on the woman.
—Vera Wang

- Take stock of what remains in your closet. Go through your pants, skirts, tops, jackets, and dresses and be impressed. Everything here should fit and look good on you.
- You put a few new outfits together with items you already own. How many new outfits did you create?
- How many days could you dress with what is in your closet today? How many different types of occasions could you dress for?
- Write a few notes about what you discovered today.

Re-evaluate, Part 2: What Do You Need?

In this manner, therefore, pray:
Our Father in heaven,
Hallowed be Your name.
Your kingdom come.
Your will be done
On earth as it is in heaven.
Give us this day our daily bread.
And forgive us our debts,
As we forgive our debtors.
And do not lead us into temptation,
But deliver us from the evil one.
For Yours is the kingdom and the power and the glory forever.
Amen.

MATTHEW 6:9–13

Today will be a fun day. Now that you've organized and created new outfits with what you already own, it's time to decide what's missing. Every wardrobe needs certain basics to build outfits upon, and also fun, creative pieces to express personality. Sometimes it's easy to get stuck in a rut when shopping, and only buy the fun, expressive pieces rather than the basic, boring ones. And sometimes, when a piece fits well and gives great service, it's easy to wear it out rather than take a risk and buy a new piece to replace it.

Now that those worn-out basics are removed from your closet, you can more easily assess what needs to be added back in. So take a look at your pants selection. Do you still have the basic dress pants you need? Do you still have the jeans you need? Follow the same pattern for tops, dresses, sweaters, and jackets. Make sure the basics are all there. If you're not sure what constitutes the basics, check out the appendix in the back of this book for a skeleton list.

Now take another look. Is your closet full of basics without much personal flair? Since you organized by color, it's easy to see if your favorites are represented. If you love color, is your wardrobe colorful? Do you see more black than any other color? Do you see many lighter or brighter colors, or is your wardrobe more somber and dark?

Another area to make note of is whether or not your accessories go with your clothes. Do your scarves relate to the clothes hanging in your closet? Choose one scarf. How many different items can you wear it with? Do you own some tops or jackets that need a little something extra at the neckline? One of my favorite tops has a neckline that is not flattering on me at all. But a scarf, or the right necklace, makes a huge difference.

Do you have the shoes you need now? Does every outfit in your closet have a pair (or pairs) of shoes to wear with it? Dress pants need heels, either on booties or pumps.

Ankle pants can be worn with pumps or flats. Bootcut jeans need boots. Slim-cut jeans can be worn with boots or flats or pumps, depending on the top. Everyone needs a good pair of athletic shoes. And of course, summer calls for different shoes than winter. Do you see any orphan shoes in your closet? You might be thinking of shoes without mates, but I also consider pairs of shoes with no coordinating clothes as orphans. Maybe you have a gorgeous pair of dressy sandals, but nothing in your closet that goes with them. Consider whether you'd rather shop for that outfit or part with the shoes.

This final assessment of your wardrobe is designed to help you fill in the gaps between what you own and what you need for a selection of outfits that express your personality and look fabulous on you. After shopping for the missing pieces, getting dressed in the morning will be easy and maybe even fun.

* * *

We've talked about the missing pieces of your wardrobe today. We spotted what wasn't there by examining what was. In other words, we had to take careful stock of the pieces we already have in order to discover what needs to be added. As we study our closets and their contents, the gaps become evident.

The same is true in our spiritual lives. Sometimes we focus more on reading the Bible and less on prayer, or the other way around. Sometimes we do what's basic and necessary, but after our obligatory fifteen minutes, we're out the door and on to the next item on our agenda. We fail to remember and ponder the truth from our quiet time throughout the day.

During certain seasons of my life, I've been so overwhelmed with cares that I can only cry out, "Jesus, help me!" I have no other words. These are the times when the Lord comes alongside and comforts me. I rest in the knowledge that the Holy Spirit is praying the right words and filling in the gaps for me.

Other seasons are so joyful, I find myself singing worship songs in my head throughout the day. But I flit from one thing to another, unable to concentrate on my Bible reading. However, the reading and study I've done in the past comes to mind to support and undergird my flightiness. Many times worship songs are based on Bible passages, and I suddenly remember how the whole verse goes because I committed it to memory in the past.

Sometimes I have long stretches when I'm burdened and need to spend much time in prayer. I'm driven to my knees. I will read short passages of Scripture, but most of my daily quiet time is spent pouring out my heart to God.

Balance can be difficult to maintain, and I often struggle to keep it. But ideally, each day we will spend time reading the Bible, listening for a word from the Holy Spirit, and praying through our concerns. This balance, like any other worthy pursuit, develops over time, through consistent, intentional effort. I often fail. But when I do, I remind myself to begin again. It is never too late to start over. As my friend Anita Brooks says, "It's never too late for a fresh start with fresh faith." Even if we don't have an hour to spend, any amount of time is better than no time.

Writing in a journal helps me. Whatever passage I read on a given day, I jot at least one important concept or truth from it in my journal. Then I pray a praise verse back to God before praying through a list of people and topics of concern that I keep in the back of my book. By following this routine each day, when the seasons that throw me off-kilter come, I have the foundations in place to fill in the gaps.

Does your daily quiet time follow a pattern? Are there any gaps in your pattern that need to be filled?

Lord Jesus, thank you for filling in the gaps when I don't know what to pray. But also thank you for instructing us in how to pray on a regular basis. Help me as I strive to maintain a consistent, orderly prayer and Bible reading time. Help me know what is missing that I need to incorporate into this time.

- Consider your daily quiet time. Does it follow a logical plan? Do you notice any glaring gaps?

- Do you journal your prayers? Do you keep a list of people and concerns in your journal that guides your prayers?

- Write the Lord's Prayer in your notebook or journal. Then list the elements you notice that it includes. Does your daily prayer time include these elements?

Wardrobe Action

It's better to have fewer things of quality than too much expendable junk.
—Rachel Zoe

- Go through the pants section of your closet. Make a list of any you need to add.

- Do the same for each section of your clothes.

- Make sure your list includes all the basics, and at least a few fun pieces.

What Does It Cost?

"If anyone comes to Me and does not hate his father and mother, wife and children, brothers and sisters, yes, and his own life also, he cannot be My disciple. And whoever does not bear his cross and come after Me cannot be My disciple. For which of you, intending to build a tower, does not sit down first and count the cost, whether he has enough to finish it—lest, after he has laid the foundation, and is not able to finish, all who see it begin to mock him, saying, 'This man began to build and was not able to finish'? Or what king, going to make war against another king, does not sit down first and consider whether he is able with ten thousand to meet him who comes against him with twenty thousand? Or else, while the other is still a great way off, he sends a delegation and asks conditions of peace. So likewise, whoever of you does not forsake all that he has cannot be My disciple. Salt is good; but if the salt has lost its flavor, how shall it be seasoned? It is neither fit for the land nor for the dunghill, but men throw it out. He who has ears to hear, let him hear!"

LUKE 14:26–35

Today we need to address a practical but not very fun topic. The list you made yesterday will cost money when you purchase the items on it. We need to discuss how much money is available and how to make it cover everything on your list.

I'm not a budget thinker. I live within the bounds of what I have, but I prefer to avoid a strict budget. I like the freedom to buy on a whim when I see just the right item. So I create categories in my budget, but I leave the details out.

For example, I know how much money is available each week to spend on food, and take time each week to list the meals we'll eat that week. I buy the ingredients for all the meals and also make sure to keep basic items on hand for a spur-of-the-moment decision to prepare a meal not listed on my weekly planner. Then I don't decide which day each meal will be eaten until that day or the day before, and I retain the freedom to add in a random, unplanned meal.

My clothing budget works the same way. I know how much I can spend each month, and I know what I need. But I retain the freedom to purchase the pair of shoes on sale that will absolutely make an older outfit new again.

However you approach your budgeting, decide how much you have to spend first. Then fill in what you'll buy. Never begin with what you need and try to make the money work, unless it is a very special occasion, such as a wedding.

And remember, you don't have to buy new or expensive things. One of my favorite local shops is a thrift store. The proprietress has a keen eye for style and shops around instead of relying only on donations. She hangs cute outfits in her windows and dresses mannequins throughout the store with drop-dead gorgeous clothes. I can always find at least one thing I need when I stop in.

Another great way to buy on a budget is to choose a

store that usually carries clothes that fit your body and your style and then get their credit card. Use it to buy groceries and other necessities like gas. Be sure to pay it off at the end of every month so you never carry a balance. You'll build up points that can be converted to cash at the clothing store. Wait for sales and then use your points. I've even gotten items for free this way. My one rule in clothes shopping is *never pay full price for anything.*

Once you have a budget in place and a strategy for shopping, you're ready to tackle your list of missing items.

* * *

Counting the cost is not only a budgetary strategy, it is also a spiritual strategy—one that Jesus taught. He told people they ought to weigh the cost before deciding to follow him.

We can imagine what it might have cost someone in the Roman Empire to follow Christ, but what about us who live in free societies? Will it cost us anything? It might. Your family might not approve. The place where you work might not allow you to speak openly about your faith. Your husband might prefer you stay home with him on Sunday rather than go to church. Your views on sexuality or freedom of speech might conflict with a coworker's.

Think about what it might cost you to be *sold out* to Jesus in the circles in which you live. Are you willing to pay the cost?

Lord Jesus, I want to be sold out to you. I want to do whatever it takes to live as your follower in every area of my life. Help me as I count the cost and assess what needs to change. I want to be salty salt.

Heart Action

- As you read the Bible passage at the beginning of this devotion, does any new thing come to mind that you need to take into account?
- Would someone else say you are *salty salt* in your social circles?
- Write out a paragraph telling what it means to you to be *sold out* to Jesus—to be salty salt.
- Does this paragraph describe you? If not, what needs to change?
- Pray, asking God to help you be what he wants you to be in your daily life.

Wardrobe Action

Buy less, choose well.
—Vivienne Westwood

- If you don't already have a monthly budget for clothes purchases, decide how to incorporate one into your existing budget.
- Create a strategy for acquiring the missing items on yesterday's list.
- If you're married, talk about your budget with your husband. He needs to agree with your planned expenditures and your strategies. (My husband loves that I know how to get *free* clothes! And he loves how my clothing choices reflect my personality and are stylish.)

Two Heads Are Better Than One

A friend loves at all times.

PROVERBS 17:17

Do you prefer to shop alone? For me, it depends on what I'm shopping for. If I need foundations, I need to be by myself. I don't enjoy this kind of shopping, and it's sort of like a trip to the dentist—I don't need anybody watching. But when it comes to shopping for other items, it can be very helpful to bring a friend along. My confidence meter rises when I'm with a friend who will give me her honest opinion. Besides, there's nothing like the camaraderie of a shopping trip between friends.

The nice thing about studying my wardrobe and making a list of needed items in advance is that it prevents me from binge shopping, or doing what is commonly referred to as *retail therapy*. We all know the thrill of discovering the perfect item, and there's nothing wrong with it when we've planned a purchase—or even when we haven't planned that particular purchase but we've been on the lookout for a fun item within our planned shopping strategy. But binge shopping outside any plan can be dangerous. It can become a psychological crutch that ruins a person financially. So stick with your plan. And by all means, bring along a girlfriend.

I am a personal shopper. I go shopping with other women to help them make decisions about style. I love to help other people spend their money! But seriously, many women love to take me along. It gives them a sense of security about their choices when I agree. And I am able to point them away from potentially disastrous clothing choices.

But any good girlfriend can do what I do, as long as she can be honest. You, as the shopper, must allow honest feedback. If your friend tells you she thinks you could do better with something else, listen to her. You might have fallen in love with the item and think you have to have it anyway. If that happens, take a breath and shop around some more. If after more shopping you still can't get the item out of your mind, and nothing else you see seems to fit the spot in your wardrobe, then go for it. Friends are not always right—just most of the time.

When I get to the point where I need several items, and I've saved within my budget for them, I call a friend. I choose one I might not have spent enough time with lately. And I make sure to choose one who loves clothes and shopping. We set a day and time, and make an event out of it. Many great memories have been made on shopping trip days. And many memories will stay between the two of us forever, because what happens on shopping trips can bond two women for a lifetime.

Remember our discussion about how Jesus calls you his friend? Often one is older and more mature than the other in a friendship. Our friendship with Jesus is like this because we're not equals with him. He is the older, more mature one. This means we can ask him for counsel and learn from his ways.

It also pleases him when we bring other friends along. Matthew 18:20 tells us, "For where two or three are gathered together in My name, I am there in the midst of them." How wonderful to know that Jesus actually comes into our presence when we gather with friends to worship and pray. There is incredible power in this kind of gathering.

You might think church is where a group gathers together for worship and prayer. But it happens in more informal gatherings too. I have some friends in another state who get together with two other couples once a month. They bring a potluck dinner and visit over the food. Then they move into a time of prayer. This group of friends has prayed together for over twenty years. The stories they tell of prayers answered in amazing ways, lives changed, and peace filling their own lives are incredible.

I am part of a group of three women who pray together. We live in three different states, and our communication is most often by text. But we call ourselves the rope of three strands that cannot be broken. With the prayer of three in agreement, we cannot be broken, no matter what stuff happens.

Jesus, thank you for being my friend. Thank you for being there for me all the time, and loving me.

Heart Action

- Create a date with Jesus. Plan a time to spend in Bible study and prayer that is longer than your normal daily time and outside your daily routine. Make it a special time by location, or study content. Make it a memory by taking a photo or making a craft.

- Are you part of a small group of friends who meet to pray? If not, ask the Lord to show you with whom he might want you to form a prayer group. Write their names here.

- Who is the girlfriend you are closest to and who will be a good prayer partner for you? Write her name here.

Wardrobe Action

Beauty is a radiance that originates from within and comes from inner security and strong character.
—Jane Seymour

- Choose a friend to shop with you. Set a date and make it an event. Be sure to take your list along. And be on the lookout for a random, fun piece.

Your Stunning Style

The Lord has heard my supplication;
The Lord will receive my prayer.

PSALM 6:9

You have reached the final day of our time together. You've cleaned out, picked up, and organized your wardrobe into a beautiful rainbow of colors that look good on you and make you feel like a million dollars. Your closet has become a thing of beauty, and so have you.

But if your closet still doesn't feel pretty, even with the pretty clothes you can now see hanging so neatly, consider making it reflect your personality like your wardrobe does. Try painting the walls your favorite color, or adding wallpaper. I realize this means you'll need to take everything out and then put it all back. But now that you know where everything goes, it won't be so hard. And just think how much more you'll enjoy your closet if the walls are attractive.

You might also consider the lighting. Is there enough light? Are the fixtures pleasing? Maybe a mini-chandelier is just what you need, or some stick-on LED lights for dark corners.

Also, there is one more way in which your closet can benefit you. It can become a place of prayer. Now that it's organized, it is a space you probably enjoy entering. If yours is a walk-in closet, this new purpose can be easily accommodated. Simply find a small, pretty chair to place in the back. Tuck a basket beside your chair containing your Bible, journal, pen, and any other materials you use daily in your quiet time.

If your clothes closet is not deep enough to accommodate a chair, at least find a spot for your quiet time basket. Then you can carry everything you need to the location you prefer. My basket travels to the kitchen island counter.

Enjoy your *new* closet and the *new* outfits you found hiding in it. Enjoy shopping for the pieces you need to fill in the gaps. Revel in your style makeover. And remember, your style is stunning just because it's yours.

* * *

You may be wondering why I suggested turning your clothes closet into the place where you pray. But I can't think of a better place to at least keep your Bible study and prayer materials. Your closet is the most intimate room in the house. It is the one place your own personality shines. Every item in your closet was chosen by you and kept because it expresses a bit of you. Hopefully, your private time with the Lord has also become better curated in the last thirty days. The two go hand in hand.

The Bible recognizes this idea too. It must have been common practice for the disciples to go into their closets to pray. Matthew 6:6 says, "But you, when you pray, go into your room, and when you have shut your door, pray to your

Father who is in the secret place; and your Father who sees in secret will reward you openly." The King James Version uses the word *closet* instead of the word *room*. I'm guessing New Testament-era houses didn't have walk-in closets just for robes and turbans, but they evidently had small rooms where one could go to be alone. The only other small room in a modern house where one can be alone besides a clothes closet is the bathroom. And the bathroom isn't really conducive to prayer and Bible study.

I suggested a basket to hold your quiet time materials. You may prefer a box of some sort. But whatever you choose, make it a compact size that is easily carried. Also make sure it is pretty. Add a little bouquet of silk flowers to one side, or paint it a pleasing color. Just make sure it isn't too utilitarian looking. You want it to look inviting.

The whole point here is that you be drawn into your quiet time by the materials and space you choose, as well as by the prospect of time spent with your best friend and mentor. And that it be a place where you can spend uninterrupted time alone. Because your makeover has just begun.

Everyone in your life has noticed some changes in your wardrobe style by now, and those closest to you have probably noticed other changes brought about by your refreshed personal time with the Lord. Life is not static, so these changes are only the beginning of some wonderful directions your life will take. Celebrate with a little party in your quiet time today.

Thank you, Lord Jesus, that you have heard all my prayers. You listen and answer when I call upon you. I can trust you with my most private concerns. You are worthy to be praised. I will celebrate your love and care over me, today.

Heart Action

- What are your most private concerns right now? Can you whisper them in the solitude of your closet?

- Do you recognize the changes that God has worked in your life in the last thirty days? Write down what you notice.

- Thank Jesus for these things.

- Play a praise song on your phone or other device and sing along. Clap your hands.

Wardrobe Action

*Nothing makes a woman more beautiful
than the belief that she is beautiful.*
—Sophia Loren

- If your closet needs sprucing up, decide on a color to paint the walls or a wallpaper print to hang. Make your notes here.

- Check out the lighting and decide on the appropriate changes, if needed. Note those here.

- If you have room for a small chair, do you already own one you can use, or do you need to look for a new one? Remember, it can be simply new to you.

- Design a basket or box for your quiet-time materials and make a home for it in your closet.

Basic Wardrobe Essentials

- A pair of denim jeans with plain pockets, in a dark wash
- A pair of casual, fun denim jeans
- A pair of black trousers (dress pants)
- Two or three pairs of shorts or casual ankle-length pants
- A knee-length pencil skirt
- A basic black dress
- Two or three shells, tank tops, or nice tees in neutral colors
- Two or three tops in fun colors
- A white blouse
- A denim jacket
- A long, lightweight cardigan sweater without buttons
- A shrug sweater

- A button-down cardigan sweater
- A pair of dressy heels
- A pair of low-heel shoes
- A pair of sandals or dressy flip-flops
- A pair of running or walking shoes
- Ankle-high booties
- Knee-high boots
- A large, beautiful scarf
- Several necklaces in gold, rose gold, and silver
- Earrings in each metal
- Three bracelets that can be worn together
- A right-hand ring

About the Author

Kathryn Graves believes genuine beauty comes only from the Creator living within, and she seeks to lead women and girls to the source of the beauty.

A pastor's wife for more than thirty years and a CLASS graduate, she also spent twelve years as a beauty and fashion expert with Premier Designs. She is the mother of two sons and has two daughters-in-law and one grandson. She loves to play with color, both in interior design and clothing fashion, and she is a pastel artist. Kathryn is the director of the crisis pregnancy ministry of her church, teaches a weekly women's Bible class, and sings on the church praise team.

"Chasing Beautiful," Kathryn's brand tag, indicates her desire to lead women on a healthy quest for both physical and spiritual well-being. Her role as pastor's wife and her BA in psychology equip her to walk alongside women who are in emotional or spiritual turmoil, leading them to the Bible for answers and hope. Kathryn's personal battle with breast cancer enables her to understand and empathize with others who suffer.

A speaker for Stonecroft Ministries' Christian Women's Clubs on the topics of fashion and finding your worth in Christ, Kathryn also serves as keynote speaker for women's banquets.

She has written devotions and articles for CBN.com, *Thriving Families*, *Clubhouse*, and Comfort-Cafe.net, and contributed stories to two books. Drama Ministry published five comedy sketches Kathryn wrote, and she is also the author of the Bible study *Beautiful Feet: A Day Spa for Your Soul*, which is designed to draw women into a deeper, more beautiful relationship with God.

Kathryn also writes material for and leads women's retreats. These retreats include the topics: "Beautiful Feet: A Prayer Make-Over," "Beautiful Treasure: A Hunt for Treasures That Last," and "Chasing Beautiful."

Find Kathryn's blog "Chasing Beautiful" at www.KathrynGraves.com.